DANIEL R. STREET

Fake News Exposed about Trump

25 of the Worst Media Lies and Biased Attacks on President Trump and His Family, Volume One

First edition

ISBN: 978-1-7379367-4-9

This book was professionally typeset on Reedsy.
Find out more at reedsy.com

Contents

Preface   v

1   2016 POLLS TELL US TRUMP CANNOT WIN   1

2   2020 POLLS TELL US TRUMP CANNOT WIN, AGAIN   10

3   TRUMP ONLY LISTENS TO BAD POLLSTERS?   20

4   COVID VACCINE BY THE END OF 2020? NO WAY   27

5   TRUMP THREATENS DEMOCRACY BY REFUSING TO ACCEPT THE ELECTION...   32

6   THE FIRST LADY BROKE HOSPITAL RULES BY READ-ING TO CHILDREN...   43

7   CAPITOL POLICE OFFICER DIES FROM HEAD TRAUMA SUSTAINED IN...   48

8   TRUMP INCITED VIOLENCE IN HIS JAN. 6 SPEECH   56

9   TRUMP WAITED 187 MINUTES TO CALL FOR PEACE ON JAN. 6?   66

10   GOP REP INSTRUCTED VP OVERTURN THE ELECTION?   72

11   TEN PEOPLE DIED IN THE JAN. 6 RIOT?   79

12   7 HOURS OF WHITE HOUSE CALL LOGS ARE MISSING?   87

13   JAN. 6 RIOTERS TOOK ZIP TIES INTO CAPITOL TO TAKE LAWMAKERS...   94

14   $30 MILLION IN DAMAGE WAS DONE BY JAN. 6 RIOT?   99

15   JAN. 6 WAS AN "ARMED INSURRECTION" TO "OVER-THROW THE...   104

16   TRUMP SAYS "HANG MIKE PENCE" IS "COMMON SENSE?"   116

17   TRUMP CANCELED THE WHITE HOUSE COMMENT LINE?   124

18   HUNTER BIDEN LAPTOP STORY IS "RUSSIAN DISINFORMATION?"   128

19   NO ONE PROFITED LIKE TRUMP AFTER LEAVING OFFICE?   139

20 TRUMP AND DESANTIS ARE FEUDING?   145

21 TRUMPS CLAIMS ABOUT WINDMILLS ARE WRONG?   150

22 TRUMP STORMED OUT OF AN INTERVIEW WITH
   PIERS MORGAN?   157

23 TRUMP SAID AMERICANS HAVE NO RIGHT TO
   PROTEST HIM?   161

24 SENATE COMMITTEE INVESTIGATING TRUMP ASSOCIATES?   165

25 TRUMP EPA CLEARS PESTICIDE AFTER MEETING
   WITH DOW CHEMICAL...   169

26 Conclusion   175

About the Author   177

Preface

Conservatives know how unfair, biased and dishonest the news media often is towards Republicans. I came of age in the Reagan-Bush era and watched daily as the news media tried to spin, hustle and lie about President Ronald Reagan and his Administration. Long before Donald Trump ran for office, I learned the media tilts to the left, towards Democrat candidates and would often twist, contort and misrepresent the news, and virtually any available story, in a brazen, transparent effort to help Democrat candidates or positions.

Therefore, like many Americans, I held a healthy distrust of the media decades before anyone ever heard of Trump Derangement Syndrome (TDS). Still, as I watched the race for the Republican Presidential nomination play out in 2015 and early 2016, I witnessed the usual leftist, biased media become absolutely frenzied. They relentlessly pummeled then-candidate Trump with phony, biased or distorted stories, broadcasts and sound bites. Many of the pundits, reporters and TV media personalities addressed Trump's campaign with thinly veiled disdain or derision. Eventually, I realized the media wanted to kill Trump's candidacy in favor of the one of the GOP establishment candidates. The fact the media wanted to bury Donald Trump's candidacy beneath a heap of GOP-E candidates piqued my interest. I started paying closer attention.

I began taking notes and compiling information on the dishonest, biased media reports on Donald Trump, his campaign, his family and his businesses. As time passed and Fake News stories and attacks continued, I began taking more comprehensive notes and making citations to authorities and sources. I ultimately decided to organize some of these notes and sources, resulting in this book and its two companion volumes.

These books are by no means a comprehensive listing of all of the lies, distortions or misrepresentations told about President Donald J. Trump, his campaign, his family or his business by the Fake News Media. A complete catalog of that many media misrepresentations would take years to compile and write. These books are merely compilations of some of the worst illustrations of Fake News Media bias, lies and distortions.

I hope this book series, and this first volume of the series, helps people become aware of the need to inform themselves. At the very least, I hope it helps dispel Fake News Media misinformation and helps a few people (or many, many people) distrust the media, inform themselves and make up their own minds. That is literally all it takes for the Fake News Media to fail and for regular Americans ("us") to win.

The Fake News Media misinformation covered in this book is presented in no particular order, though I did attempt to group together media stories about the same topic. For instance, breakdowns of misinformation about the phony January 6, 2021 Capitol Riot and the aftermath, are presented together, for the most part. Whenever necessary, background information is provided to add context to the issues addressed by each story. As you read, you will probably marvel at how blatantly dishonest so many of the stories pushed by Fake News Media are and how many of the blatantly dishonest stories you completely forgot about amid the endless cacophony of Fake News Media misinformation.

Anyway, I hope you find my book useful, entertaining and enlightening. If you do find it a good read, I hope you will read Volumes Two and Three of the series.

Please visit my website, DanielRStreet.com for more information about my books, for news and updates about upcoming books and more. Also, visit my substack at danielrstreet.substack.com for breakdowns of Fake News stories, Media misinformation and other nonsense of the day. Finally, please join my email list at https://www.danielrstreet.com/v1b/. Visit this link to sign up and *receive a free bonus chapter* only available to my readers. If you enjoy seeing the Media, politicians, government and industry getting called to the carpet for their misinformation campaigns, you will love all of the above.

Daniel. R. Street, Monroe, Louisiana

1

2016 POLLS TELL US TRUMP CANNOT WIN

BACKGROUND: This issue calls for some background to give the Fake News context. Polling is a time-honored tradition in the United States.Americans are bombarded daily with polls. We are peppered with polls about political topics, religion, race, politics and literally every conceivable issue in existence. Most people are aware that polls can be, and are, manipulated to reflect pre-determined results. Public opinion polling is actually supposed to report on and reflect how the American public feels about a particular topic or set of topics. Sometimes public opinion polls do just that. Other times, however, public opinion polls are illegitimately intended to *shape* and *influence* the attitudes, views and beliefs of people, rather than reflect those attitudes, views or beliefs. There are endless illustrations of this tactic with respect to public opinion polls. Deep diving into that issue would require another book altogether (there is an idea).

Political election polling and surveys, on the other hand, are supposed to inform the public or a paper or news outlet's readers or a political campaign about the voting intentions and support of voters. Regarding Presidential Elections, the polls and surveys may be directed at the National Popular Vote (which is really meaningless for purposes of determining the winner of a

U.S. Presidential race), while others are directed at the support and voter preferences in individual states. Forecast modeling generally predicts the results of elections. With respect to Presidential elections, some forecast models predict popular vote totals, some predict Electoral College results, some predict state-by-state results, etc...

Remember, in the United States of America the popular vote does not determine the next President. The Founding Fathers did not want the Presidential election to be strictly a nationwide popularity contest, as that would grant more populous States too much influence. To offset the sheer numbers of more populous States, the United States Constitution created a Presidential Election system based on slates of Electors from each State.The Presidency is determined by what amounts to 50 Statewide contests. (Technically, when we vote for president we are actually voting for a particular candidate's slate of electors.) The winner of each State basically gets awarded that State's electors. Each State's electors are the sum of the seats each State holds in the United States House of Representatives (where seats are apportioned based on population share) and Senators (where each State has 2). A total of 270 Electoral Votes are needed to win the election.

Most of the 2016 Presidential polls, surveys and forecast models wrongly projected and predicted a resounding Hillary Clinton victory. This is particularly true regarding much of the State-by-State data (which is infinitely more meaningful than national popular vote data, since the national popular vote does not determine the winner of a Presidential Election). To many observers and voters these "incorrect" prognostications were not mistakes, but rather, represented efforts to influence the outcome of the election in favor of Hillary Clinton. Stated another way, many polls, surveys and forecasts were Fake News. With this background in mind, let's take a look at the Fake News surrounding 2016 U.S. Presidential Election polling, surveys and forecast modeling.

THE FAKE NEWS

Presidential polls, surveys and forecasts in 2016 projected Hillary Clinton would be the winner of the United States Presidential Election.

Who Pushed the Fake News?

Virtually every news outlet and polling outfit in the Country, with only a handful of exceptions, declared Hillary Clinton would win the 2016 election and gave Donald Trump nearly no chance to win. This was done through the use of polling data, forecast models and surveys. Some of the most notable erroneous predictions are noted below.

The New York Times gave Hillary Clinton an 85% chance of winning the 2016 election based on its polling data as of November 8, 2016. See *nytimes.com*.

The *Princeton Election Consortium* placed Hillary Clinton's probability of being elected President at 99% as of November 6, 2016. See *election.princeton.edu*:

All estimates point toward HRC>50% probability. What determines the exact number?

On November 2, 2016, *The Independent* in the United Kingdom reported *Moody's Analytics* predicted an "easy" Hillary Clinton win with 332 Electoral College votes to Donald Trump's 206 Electoral College votes. See *indepen-dent.co.uk*: (Readers will recall 270 Electoral College votes are needed for a candidate to win the election.)

Prediction model that has correctly picked every US president since 1980 says Hillary Clinton will easily win

Sabato's Crystal Ball at the UVA Center for Politics predicted an Electoral

College blowout for Hillary Clinton with her winning over Trump 322 to 216. See *centerforpolitics.org*, November 7, 2016:

Our Final 2016 picks

Clinton 322, Trump 216; 50-50 Senate; GOP holds House

Nate Silver at *FiveThirtyEight* gave Hillary Clinton a 71.4% to chance to win the 2016 election to Donald Trump's 28.6% chance. See *https://projects.fivethirtyeight.com/2016-election-forecast.*

Reuters/Ipsos gave Hillary Clinton a 90% chance of winning the election as of November 7, 2016. See *reuters.com*:

Clinton has 90 percent chance of winning: Reuters/Ipsos States of the Nation

A review of some of the notable polls issued very close to Election Day illustrate the Fake News:

Survey Monkey's Florida poll, based on polling data compiled from November 1, 2016 through November 7, 2016, had Hillary Clinton up in Florida 51% to 42%. See *nytimes.com* (interactive 2016 elections polling).

Quinnipiac University's Florida poll, based on polling data compiled from November 3, 2016 through November 6, 2016, had Hillary Clinton up in Florida by 1 point. See *nytimes.com* (interactive 2016 elections polling).

Survey Monkey's North Carolina poll, based on polling data compiled from November 1, 2016 through November 7, 2016 had Hillary Clinton up 49% to 41%. See *nytimes.com* (interactive 2016 elections polling).

Survey Monkey's New Hampshire poll, based on polling data compiled from November 1, 2016 through November 7, 2016 had Hillary Clinton up 49% to 37%. See *nytimes.com* (interactive 2016 elections polling).

UNH/WMUR's New Hampshire poll, based on polling data compiled from November 3, 2016 through November 6, 2016 had Hillary Clinton up 49% to 38%. See *nytimes.com* (interactive 2016 elections polling).

Ipsos/Reuters' Pennsylvania poll, based on polling data compiled from October 17, 2016 to November 6, 2016, had Hillary Clinton up 48% to 45%. See *nytimes.com* (interactive 2016 elections polling).

Franklin & Marshall College's Pennsylvania poll, with one week to go before the election, had Hillary Clinton up 49% to 38%. See *fandm.edu.*

UPI/CVoter's Wisconsin poll, based on polling data compiled from October 30, 2016 to November 6, 2016 had Hillary Clinton up 51% to 43%. See *nytimes.com* (interactive 2016 elections polling).

Ipsos/Reuters' Minnesota poll, based on polling data compiled from October 17, 2016 to November 6, 2016, had Hillary Clinton up 44% to 36%. See *nytimes.com* (interactive 2016 elections polling).

The Wrap published a good article on November 9, 2016, highlighting many of these egregious errors. See *thewrap.com*, "*Here's Every Major Poll That Got Donald Trump's Election Win Wrong.*"

THE TRUTH

Of course, Donald Trump won the 2016 U.S. Presidential Election, but you do not need a source to be cited to know that. A closer look at the results will illustrate the errors made by the so-called "experts."

Donald Trump won the Electoral College with 306 electoral college votes to Hillary Clinton's 232. See *Politico.com* (2016 election results).

Contrary to Survey Monkey's polling predicting Donald Trump would lose Florida by 8%, Donald Trump won the State of Florida by 119,770 votes or by 1.3%. See *Politico.com* (2016 election results).

Contrary to Ipsos/Reuters' polling which predicted Donald Trump would lose Pennsylvania by 3%, Donald Trump won Pennsylvania by 68,236 votes. See *Politico.com* (2016 election results).

Contrary to UPI/CVoter's polling which predicted Donald Trump would lose Wisconsin by 8%, Donald Trump won Wisconsin by 27,257 votes. See *Politico.com* (2016 election results).

Contrary to Survey Monkey's polling which predicted Donald Trump would lose North Carolina by 8%, Donald Trump won North Carolina by over 177,000 votes. See *Politico.com* (2016 election results).

Additionally, several of the States won by Hillary Clinton were won by much narrower margins than the so-called "experts" predicted.

UNH/WMUR's New Hampshire poll predicted Hillary Clinton would win the State by a margin of 11% in 2016. In fact, Hillary Clinton won New Hampshire by 2,732 votes. See *Politico.com* (2016 election results). (And Clinton may have eked out that win with some help from illegal out-of-state votes. See *Breitbart.com*, "*Exclusive – Kobach: It Appears That out-of-State Voters Changed the Outcome of the New Hampshire U.S. Senate Race,*" September 7, 2017 and *nhpr.org*, "*Couple Pleads Guilty to Voting in N.H. And Mass. During 2016 Election,*" December 18, 2019.)

An Ipsos/Reuters poll had Hillary Clinton winning Minnesota by 8%. In fact, Hillary Clinton won Minnesota by less than 44,000 votes or 1.5%. See

Politico.com (2016 election results).

I could continue, but hopefully the point is made. Much of the State-by-State polling, survey and forecast data was dead wrong in 2016. Furthermore, the publication and dissemination of these polls shortly before the election could influence the outcome. A Trump voter in Wisconsin, for instance, might see the UPI/CVoter poll showing Hillary Clinton with an 8% lead only two days before the election and stay home. Simply put, the polls and forecasts were Fake News.

Commentary: This chapter outlines just a smattering of the polling, forecast and survey errors which occurred in 2016. There were many more. In fact, I could recite erroneous poll after erroneous poll for the 2016 Presidential Election for pages on end. (For those interested in delving deeper into the wild polling errors in 2016, go to the *RealClearPolitics.com*, "Battle for the White House" page where one may pull up the State-by-State polling and election results. That is a good place to start, though far from the final word.) The point is many of these polls, forecasts and surveys were not only off, they were way off. They were so far off to the point they could easily be considered propaganda. What is most telling, or troubling, is the lack of circumspection among some in the industry and Fake News Media about the 2016 polling. Nate Silver, the forecast modeler behind *FiveThirtyEight* and once (at least) widely regarded among political prognosticators, penned an article informing the American people that *"The Polls Are All Right"* on May 30, 2018 on his website *fivethirtyeight.com*. Another good illustration of this way of thinking is found in an article published by *The Hill* on January 19, 2017, entitled, *"One last look: 2016 polls actually got a lot right."* See *thehill.com*.

Expounding on this mentality, one paper evaluating the accuracy of 2016 Presidential Election surveys concluded *"... the problem was the incorrect interpretation of the survey results, not the initial data collection. Meaning the fault, if any exists, lies with consumers of science, not with the producers. Therefore, the solution is for laypeople, such as journalists who published the polls, and the*

7

audience who closely followed the polls, to change their general attitude toward, and relationship with surveys." See *Oak Ridge Institute for Science and Education, orise.orau.gov, "Surveying the Science: 'Fixing' the 2016 Election Polls."* Given the pervasiveness of this mentality in the industry, one would not expect much, if any, improvement in results in the future.

Ironically, much of this polling "apologist" mentality is premised on the relatively less inaccurate (but still off) national polling, as opposed to the more erroneous State-by-State results (despite the fact national vote doesn't decide the race), and historical analysis claiming the 2016 results really were not much worse than other Presidential election cycles. Stated another way, much of the polling "apologist" mentality excuses the hideous results in 2016 by claiming the results were not so bad regarding the measure by which the election is not decided (the national popular vote, though the pollsters and modelers missed that too in 2016) and by claiming the polls/surveys/models are generally poor every time. You probably are not very comforted by that mentality and you should not be.

Always keep in mind the Fake News Media cannot stop spreading misinformation. They literally cannot help themselves. This the-polls-are-just-fine nonsense is a good illustration. Anyone old enough to remember the polling and predictions leading up to the 2016 Presidential Election knows full well how the entire Fake News Media, government and political establishment were absolutely convinced Hillary Clinton had the election in the bag. They were all literally in shock when she lost. They drank their own "cool aid" and believed their own lies. The polls, forecasts and election surveys were the foundation of those lies and they were wrong to the point of being literal misinformation.

Thus, much of the Fake News establishment needed to convince people 2016 polling was actually not poor at all to justify their continued existence and relevance or, possibly, because future efforts to influence the 2020 election (or other elections) might not prove effective otherwise. As I mentioned above, some of these polls may have influenced the election. There is, in fact, some scientific basis to believe polling does influence elections. The notion that polling, particularly polling strongly favoring one candidate, may cause voters to support the winning candidate is known in the industry as the "bandwagon effect" or "contagion effect." See *Do Polls Influence the Vote, Capturing Campaign Effects*, University of Michigan Press (2006); *The Bandwagon Curve, American Journal of Political Science*, Vol. 21, No. 4 (Nov. 1977); *Experimental Studies of the Impact of Poll Results on Electoral Behavior, Political Communication*, Vol. 11 (1994) *and Are Public Opinion Polls Self-Fulfilling Prophecies?, Research and Politics*, July–September 2014. There are many more studies confirming the "bandwagon effect" which polling can create, but these are enough to get a curious reader started.

(To be fair, some studies also show a potential "underdog effect" where some voters are apparently motivated to vote for the candidate trailing in the polls. See *Public Reactions to Polling News during the 1988 Presidential Election Campaign, Polling and Presidential Election Coverage* (1991).)

The data on the "bandwagon effect" has been around for decades and no doubt the Fake News Media peddlers are well familiar with it. The manner in which they elevated and promoted Hillary Clinton and anything indicating she would win the election certainly creates the impression they were aware of it and actively worked to ensure a Clinton victory. At least, one might easily reach such conclusions.

Nevertheless, if the polls, forecasts and surveys were in fact relatively accurate and were NOT misinformation, one would expect their predictions to be more accurate in 2020 right? The next chapter of this book tells that tale.

2

2020 POLLS TELL US TRUMP CANNOT WIN, AGAIN

The 2020 Presidential Polls and Surveys were propaganda, again.

THE FAKE NEWS

In 2020 political polling, forecasting and surveying will be more accurate than in 2016 and this time Trump does not have a chance.

Who Pushed the Fake News?

Business Insider published an article on July 20, 2020, entitled, *"The presidential polls in 2016 weren't as wrong you think. Here's why you can trust them in 2020."* See *businessinsider.com.* The article downplays the errors in 2016 and informs the reader that 2020 is very different because of the pandemic, because Joe Biden is liked better than Hillary Clinton and for other reasons:

The presidential polls in 2016 weren't as wrong you think. Here's why you can trust them in 2020.

Vox assured the public, in an article published on October 28, 2020, the polls and forecast models could be trusted this time around, because "Today's forecasts built in more GOP-friendly assessments of state dynamics" and because the "modeling has improved." See *vox.com*:

Biden has a big lead in the polls, but can we trust them?

FiveThirtyEight surveyed pollsters in 2020 and found "nearly every pollster we talked to has made some kind of modification since the last general election. Some changes were precipitated by what happened in 2016..." See *"What Pollsters Have Changed Since 2016 – And What Still Worries Them About 2020,"* October 13, 2020, *fivethirtyeight.com*. (Wait, but Nate Silver with 538 told us there was nothing to fix after 2016, right? See *"The Polls Are All Right"* on May 30, 2018, *fivethirtyeight.com*. Apparently, pollsters disagreed since they "made changes.") At any rate, this 2020 article went on to outline some of the changes in weighting and methodology employed in 2020 by various different polling outfits and forecasters.

A *Pacific University* article published on October 12, 2020, entitled, *"In 2020, Presidential Polling is More Reliable Than in 2016, Says Politics Professor Jim Moore,"* *pacificu.edu*, quoted Professor Jim Moore, director of political outreach at The Pacific University of Oregon Tom McCall Center for Civic Engagement, who comforted readers telling them "The polling is better this time. You can trust it more." The basis for the new trust was pollsters were factoring education levels and gender more and paying more attention to state races.

Cook Political Report in a web post made on July 10, 2020, assured readers with the following caption, *"The Polls Weren't Far off in 2016. They Aren't Wrong Now, Either."* See *cookpolitical.com*:

The Polls Weren't Far off in 2016. They Aren't Wrong Now, Either.

Newsweek weighed in on the topic on September 18, 2020, with *"How the Pollsters Changed Their Game After Getting the 2016 Election Wrong."* See *newsweek.com*. This article, again, touted the changes made by most pollsters in how they factored education levels as a substantial improvement in methodology.

Similar citations could be listed endlessly to further confirm the industry claims that all was well on the polling front as the United States headed into the 2020 Presidential Election, but hopefully, the point is made.

The modelers, however, persisted with their predictions decisively in favor of the Democrat Party Presidential Nominee, this time Joe Biden.

The Economist forecast model gave Joe Biden a 97% chance of winning the Electoral College.

Fivethirtyeight gave Joe Biden an 89% chance of winning the election.

(In 2020, *The New York Times* decided not to provide an estimate of the chances of each candidate to win the Presidential Election. The paper's excuse? According to the NYT the "short version: mail voting." See *nytimes.com*, *"Needle Update: What to Expect on Election Night."* Perhaps, the paper was actually embarrassed enough by its wildly erroneous 2016 prediction to take a pass on guessing about 2020.)

As of Election Day 2020, *the fivethirtyeight* (again, Nate Silver's forecast modeling website) average of the following State's Presidential Election polls had President Trump or Joe Biden up by the following percentages:

(The data cited below is from the *fivethirtyeight.com* 2020 Presidential general election polls for each respective state found at *https://projects.fivethirtyeight.com/polls/president-general/2020*):

Pennsylvania - Joe Biden up by 4.7%.

Florida - Joe Biden up by 2.5%.

Wisconsin - Joe Biden up by 8.4%.

North Carolina — Joe Biden up by 1.8%.

Texas — Donald Trump up by 1.1%.

Ohio — Donald Trump up by .8%.

Iowa — Donald Trump up by 1.3%.

Missouri — Donald Trump up by 8.0%.

(Keep in mind the percentages cited above are AVERAGES of multiple polling results from various different polling entities.)

Some prominent individual polls are worth mentioning here.

As *The Hill* loudly trumpeted in the weeks leading up to Election Day on November 3, 2020, Quinnipiac had Joe Biden ahead of President Trump in Florida by 11 points. See *thehill.com*, *"Biden holds 11-point lead over Trump in Florida in new Quinnipiac poll."*

A Washington Post/ABC News Wisconsin poll released on October 28, 2020 (one week before the election) found Joe Biden with a 17 point lead over President Trump, 57% to 40%. See *U.S. News & World Report*, *"Biden Opens*

Gaping 17-point Lead on Trump in Wisconsin, Poll Finds," usnews.com.

A Monmouth University Pennsylvania poll released the day before the election gave Joe Biden 7 point lead, 51% to 44% on November 2, 2020. See *"Biden Holds Lead Despite Trump Gains in Swing Counties,"* Monmouth.edu.

A CNN poll of North Carolina released on October 31, 2020, just days before Election Day (November 3, 2020) gave Joe Biden a 6 point lead, 51% to 44%. See *cdn.cnn.com*.

Another Monmouth University poll, this one in Florida, released on October 29, 2020, gave Joe Biden a 6 point lead over President Trump, 51% to 45%. See *"Biden Maintains Lead,"* Monmouth.edu.

THE TRUTH

The polls were not only off in 2020, *they performed considerably worse than in 2016* and, in fact, according to a special task force convened by the *American Association for Public Opinion Research*, the 2020 pre-election polling had the largest errors in the last 40 years for the popular vote and the worst in the last 20 years for State level estimates. See *AAPOR Report* at *aapor.org*:

2020 Pre-Election Polling: An Evaluation of the 2020 General Election Polls

How did the polling averages cited above compare to the actual results? Well, let's take a look.

Again, the *FiveThirtyEight* polling averages for various states are listed below, along with the actual results. (The averages are cited first for each State, followed by the actual results. The data for the averages are from the *FiveThirtyEight.com* 2020 Presidential general election polls for each respective state found at *https://projects.fivethirtyeight.com/polls/president -general/2020* while the actual results cited to the right are from *Politico.com* (2020 election results).)

Pennsylvania:
   Joe Biden up by 4.7%. The result: Joe Biden won by 1.2%.

Florida:
   Joe Biden up by 2.5%. The result: President Trump won by 3.2%.

Wisconsin:
   Joe Biden up by 8.4%. The result: Joe Biden won by .7%.

North Carolina:
   Joe Biden up by 1.8%. The result: President Trump won by 1.4%.

Texas:
   Donald Trump up by 1.1%. The result: President Trump won by 5.6%.

Ohio:
   Donald Trump up by .8%. The result: President Trump won by 8%.

Iowa:
   Donald Trump up by 1.3%. The result: President Trump won by 8.2%.

Missouri:
   Donald Trump up by 8.0%. The result: President Trump won by 15.4%.

Not only were individual polls wildly inaccurate in many cases, the averages were oten way off the mark as noted above. Furthermore, the breakdown by *FiveThirtyEight* of the average polling error in the final 21 days for the 2020 general election (not limited to the Presidential race, but including other

Federal and State wide races) for many polling firms were abysmal.

The *FiveThirtyEight* polling error rate for the last 21 days before the 2020 general elections for selected pollsters are reproduced here:

Monmouth University 10.1%

Quinnipiac University 7.1%

Public Policy Polling 7.2%

Sienna College/NYT Upshot 5.5%

SSRS 7.7%

RMG Research 6.0%

Change Research 6.1%

See *FiveThirtyEight.com*, "*The Death Of Polling is Greatly Exaggerated. But maybe live-caller polls aren't the gold standard anymore.*" March 25, 2021. (Even after this abysmal, pathetic showing, Nate Silver is telling people the results are not so bad.)

PLEASE NOTE: Do not interpret the citations to *FiveThirtyEight* in this Chapter and the preceding Chapter as any endorsement. In fact, *FiveThirtyEight* and the architect of it, Nate Silver, are not the "Gold Standard," far from it (but that is another story altogether). Frankly, given Silver's track record and status, the averages he cites are probably quite conservative (meaning, his averages might make the pollsters look better than they should. This writer did not delve into the methodology used by Silver to arrive at the averages cited above, as that effort is beyond the scope of this book.) The fact is there are very few outfits conducting analysis such as this. What little there is does not look good.

The Quinnipiac poll giving Joe Biden an 11 point lead in Florida (see *thehill.com*, "*Biden holds 11-point lead over Trump in Florida in new Quinnipiac poll.*") shortly before the election was grossly misleading, as President Trump won the State by 2.3%.

The Washington Post/ABC News Wisconsin poll released on October 28, 2020, (one week before the election, See *U.S. News & World Report*, *"Biden Opens Gaping 17-point Lead on Trump in Wisconsin, Poll Finds,"* usnews.com), proclaiming Joe Biden had a 17 point lead over President Trump, 57% to 40%, was misinformation, as Joe Biden eked out a victory by just over 20,000 votes. (Of course, this is one of several States where Biden's "victory" is particularly suspect, but that is another story I will cover in an upcoming book.)

Importantly, the errors were not limited to the Presidential Race. As the *FiveThirtyEight* polling error article cited abovfe shows, many pollsters missed the mark on U.S. Senate and U.S. House races, as well as State Governor races. Analysis conducted by others confirms this as well.

Costas Panagopoulos, a professor of political science and chair in the Department of Political Science at Northeastern University, conducted an extensive analysis of the 2020 polling data. His conclusions are striking. See *Accuracy and Bias in the 2020 U.S. General Election Polls,"* costaspanagopoulos.com. The preamble to the report tells the story: "Overall, national and statewide polls in 2020 were considerably less accurate than in 2016. In fact, there is evidence the final, national presidential preelection polls were less accurate than in any cycle since 1996. Polls across the board underestimated Republican support in the presidential, U.S. Senate and gubernatorial races. *The results show the pro-Democratic biases reflected in the final 2020 preelection polls were systematic.*" (Emphasis added.)

The New York Post published a good article on November 13, 2020, entitled, *"Why election polls were so wrong again in 2020."* The article breaks down some of the failures of Fake News Media polls and interviews Richard Baris whose *Big Data Poll* (bigdatapoll.com) nailed Florida to within a fraction of a percentage point. Baris explains some of the issues and failures of modern polling. This article is worth reading to gain a better understanding of the problem.

Why election polls were so wrong again in 2020

In February 2022, Richard Baris made a very informative speech and presentation at Hillsdale College entitled, *Is Polling Reliable Anymore?* (The presentation was part of Hillsdale College's National Leadership Seminar series. See *freedomlibrary.hillsdale.edu.*) The answer is, in most cases, polling is NOT reliable anymore. Please take the time to watch this presentation. Mr. Baris covers the problems in polling from methodology to bias to ethics (or the lack thereof), the lack of accountability and more.It is well worth your time.

The bottom line is the pre-election polls were Fake News. Now you know.

Commentary: The Fake News Media knows full well about the "bandwagon effect." Time and again they publish and promote skewed, inaccurate, misleading or just dead wrong polling data favoring Democrat candidates. This phenomenon was on full display yet again (this time on steroids) during the 2020 Presidential election (and in the 2016 election). All of the hand-wringing and excuses bandied about by the industry analysts and experts cannot explain these repeated, system-wide failures. (Just read the Conclusion section of *Accuracy and Bias in the 2020 U.S. General Election Polls,*" *costaspanagopoulos.com.*, where the author briefly mentions some of the explanations offered by pollsters. Maybe the problem is the shy Trump voters or late deciders or differences in non-response from Trump and Biden voters, etc...)

What virtually no one, other than Richard Baris and a handful of others, mentions at all is maybe some of these errors are NOT mistakes. Maybe some of these errors are deliberate attempts to influence the outcomes of elections. Why wouldn't at least some of these outfits manipulate their numbers to influence the election? There are rarely any significant consequences to their errors, other than humiliation and loss of credibility (which none seem to care a wit about), so what is stopping them? The only profession, other than Fake News polling, where a person can be so consistently wrong and keep his or her job is weather forecasting.

Undoubtedly, some of these polling errors are honest mistakes, after all, the process is complicated and accuracy can be difficult to obtain. Maybe some of the errors, however, are not mistakes at all. Nevertheless, the fact Americans face polling and election forecasting so shoddy and so often systematically in favor of the Democrat Party is sad commentary by itself, regardless of whether the results are due to incompetence or not. Read through the first Chapter, this Chapter and Chapter three of this book and decide for yourself whether you believe all of the poor polling and election forecasting result solely from "mistakes."

3

TRUMP ONLY LISTENS TO BAD POLLSTERS?

No, but *The New York Times* does.

THE FAKE NEWS

President Trump only believes in fake polls that show him winning.

Who Pushed the Fake News?

The New York Times, of course. The NYT pushed this angle in an article published originally on November 1, 2020, entitled, *"To Trump, 'the Polls That Matter' Point to Victory. The Rest Are 'Fake.'"* See *nytimes.com:*

To Trump, 'the Polls That Matter' Point to Victory. The Rest Are 'Fake.'

The article blasts President Trump for focusing only on polls which were "good for him." According to the NYT, "Polls that show him trailing Joseph R.

Biden, Jr. – virtually all national polls – are simply 'fake news.'" (All of the following quotes and references are from this *New York Times* article.)

The article goes on to claim, "The president's blinkered view has created something of an alternate universe, one not governed by polling averages or independent analysis but by declarative statements that, at times, feel as if they are coming out of nowhere."

The NYT then claims the polls that "matter" to President Trump are *Rasmussen Reports* which, according to the NYT, "consistently – and in isolation – has a rosier picture for the president nationally than other surveys do" and *Trafalgar Group* which, again according to the NYT, "... had better number for Mr. Trump in midwestern states."

The article continues at length making several condescending and demeaning claims, including claiming the President has "shown little understanding of data science," that he treats voter support as "mystical, rather than a mathematical, proposition," and the he "makes polling a punchline," among others.

Of course, no *New York Times* article about President Trump is complete without relying on some anonymous sources and this article does not disappoint. Supposedly, President Trump's son-in-law, Jared Kushner, touted analysis done for the campaign by Matt Oczkowski, formerly with Cambridge Analytica, as showing "votes will break Mr. Trump's way in the final days of the campaign," according to *"people who have heard the comments."*

The article also claims Trump campaign analyst Brock McCleary came up with "estimates of Mr. Trump's poll standing" which are less "negative" than "some other Trump pollsters," according to *"people close to the campaign."*

The NYT also claims in the article that Republican National Committee turnout models show "Mr. Trump performing worse than he does in the campaign's own polls" in some scenarios, "two people briefed on the matter said." See *The New York Times*, "*To Trump, 'the Polls That Matter' Point to Victory. The Rest Are 'Fake,'*" November 1, 2020, *nytimes.com*.

THE TRUTH

The previous two chapters of this book lay the foundation for the truth here. Much of the State and National polling in both 2016 and 2020 was wrong to the point of being misinformation. Despite knowing how misleading the polling was in 2016 and despite the egregious error made by *The New York Times* in 2016 giving Hillary Clinton a virtual lock on winning the election, here they are days before the election in 2020 lambasting President Trump for not believing the same pitiful polls this time around.

Of course, the polling in 2020 was not just off. With respect to national polls it was the worst in 40 years and with respect to State polling it was the worst in two decades, according to the industry itself. See *American Association for Public Opinion Research* report entitled, "*2020 Pre-Election Polling: An Evaluation of General Election Polls*," at aapor.org. (This report and the issues it addresses were covered in Chapter Two.)

The pro-Democrat bias of the pre-election 2020 polls (not just the Presidential polls, but in Senate races and State gubernatorial races as well) was systematic, according to Professor Panagopoulos. See *Accuracy and Bias in the 2020 U.S. General Election Polls*," *costaspanagopoulos.com*. (Also covered in Chapter Two.)

Furthermore, the *FiveThirtyEight* polling error rate for the last 21 days before the 2020 general elections for selected pollsters were massive:

Monmouth University 10.1%
Quinnipiac University 7.1%
Public Policy Polling 7.2%

Sienna College/NYT Upshot 5.5%
SSRS 7.7%
RMG Research 6.0%
Change Research 6.1%

See *FiveThirtyEight.com*, *"The Death Of Polling is Greatly Exaggerated. But maybe live-caller polls aren't the gold standard anymore."* March 25, 2021. (Again, covered in Chapter Two.)

And those polling averages *The New York Times* ridiculed President Trump for being skeptical of? Those were way off. Some of the *FiveThirtyEight* averages and the actual results from the Presidential Election are reproduced again below. (The data for the averages are from the fivethirtyeight.com 2020 Presidential general election polls for each respective state found at *https://projects.fivethirtyeight.com/polls/president-general/2020* while the actual results cited to the right are from *Politico.com* (2020 election results).):

Pennsylvania:
Joe Biden up by 4.7%. The result: Joe Biden won by 1.2%.

Florida:
Joe Biden up by 2.5%. The result: President Trump won by 3.2%.

Wisconsin:
Joe Biden up by 8.4%. The result: Joe Biden won by .7%.

North Carolina:
Joe Biden up by 1.8%. The result: President Trump won by 1.4%.

Texas:
Donald Trump up by 1.1%. The result: President Trump won by 5.6%.

Ohio:

Donald Trump up by .8%. The result:President Trump won by 8%.

Iowa:
Donald Trump up by 1.3%. The result:President Trump won by 8.2%.

Missouri:
Donald Trump up by 8.0%. The result: President Trump won by 15.4%.

Also, which pollsters did the best in 2020? The *FiveThirtyEight* article referenced above confirms two of the very pollsters *The New York Times* ridiculed President Trump for focusing on, namely, *Rasmussen Reports* and *Trafalgar Group*, were <u>among the most accurate of the entire election cycle</u>. (Both were in the top three most accurate.)

The hubris and condescension of *The New York Times* in this article is hard to bear. One would think the paper's editors would have the decency to correct the article to reflect President Trump turned out to be right about which polls to follow and *The New York Times* and its pitiable White House Correspondent were not. No such luck. Fake News Media lacks the self-awareness or credibility to do such a thing.

<u>Commentary</u>: The self-righteous way the Fake News Media touts the polls they promote is only part of the problem. While Fake News Media often takes the we-are-more-intelligent-more-well-informed-and-superior-to-you approach to so many issues of the day, consider how the polling industry "headliners" and Fake News Media treat the most accurate polling firms. As the *New York Intelligencer* reported in an article published on March 26, 2021, entitled, *"What Did We Learn About Political Polling in 2020?"* some of the pollsters "thought to have shoddy methodologies and partisan bias . . .," were the most accurate. See *nymag.com*. According to the *New York Intelligencer*, these "partisan" pollsters with "shoddy methodologies" were *AtlasIntel*, *Trafalgar Group*, and *Rasmussen Reports* and a couple of others.

Richard Baris with *Big Data Polls* wrote a guest piece at *rasmussenreports.com* on April 5, 2019 (long before the 2020 election), outlining many of the misstatements made by the so-called industry "leaders" about maligned, but actually far more accurate pollsters (like Baris, Rasmussen, Trafalgar) and the egregious errors made by the so-called polling industry "leaders" in race after race all over the Country. This is worth a read to get just a sampling of the endless errors and persistent arrogance of some of the "leaders" in the polling industry. A review of these endless errors, known full well, no doubt, to *The New York Times* when it published the ridiculous attack on President Trump covered in this Chapter, leaves virtually anyone wondering why in the world the NYT would even broach the topic.

Much of the problem is this: just like most of the editors, reporters and broadcasters at most of the Fake News Media outlets, many of the Fake News Media pollsters are leftists who don't care for ordinary people, conservatives or most of the things ordinary people hold dear. Richard Baris made this exact point in the *Rasmussen Reports* commentary cited above. This political and ideological bent is reflected in their polling.

In many cases their "polls" are thinly veiled Democrat Party propaganda. 2020 is just another illustration of this phenomena. (Some of the 2021 polling was even worse, but that is yet another story for another time.)

Compare Richard Baris's *People's Pundit Daily* and *Big Data Polls* (https://www .peoplespunditdaily.com/latest-polls/election-2020-public-polling-project /) performance in 2020 in Florida with *Quinnipiac* (See *The Hill*, "*Biden holds 11-point lead over Trump in Florida in new Quinnipiac poll,*" October 7, 2020) or *Monmouth University* (which gave Biden a 4-6 point lead over Trump in Florida on October 29, 2020) or *Reuters/Ipsos* (which also gave Biden a 4 point lead over Trump in Florida in a survey ending on November 1, 2020). Baris had Trump winning Florida by a couple of points. Baris got it right, as President Trump won Florida by 3.3%. *Quinnipiac, Monmouth* and *Reuters/Ipsos* (just to name a few) were off. Who would you listen to? Better yet, would you ridicule

25

or attack anyone for NOT listening to the least accurate ones? Of course, not.

Do yourself a favor and skip the Fake News polling. When you want or need polling and polling data check *People's Pundit Daily* and *Big Data Polls*, *Trafalgar Group*, *Rasmussen Reports* and *AtlasIntel*. The Fake News Media might poke fun at you, but at least you won't be as likely to have egg on your chin after the election.

4

COVID VACCINE BY THE END OF 2020? NO WAY

President Trump was right again.

THE FAKE NEWS

President Trump's claims during the early stages of the COVID pandemic in 2020 that a vaccine would be available before the end of the year were wrong.

Who Pushed the Fake News?

President Trump claimed a COVID-19 vaccine would be ready for distribution by the end of 2020 numerous times throughout the year. Each time, Fake News Media responded with open skepticism or ridicule.

On May 15, 2020, in response to President Trump's claim a COVID vaccine could be ready by year's end, *ABC News* published an article entitled, "*Trump promises coronavirus vaccine by end of the year, but his own experts temper expectations.*" See *abcnews.go.com*. (Despite the title to the article, President Trump actually did not "promise" any such thing. He said the Administration was working to development "treatments and vaccines as quickly as possible . . . by the end of the year if we can." Even the headline is Fake News.)

Trump promises coronavirus vaccine by end of the year, but his own experts temper expectations

Various different experts are quoted in the ABC News article as reluctant to confirm such an expeditious timeline, with a few questioning whether the time line is possible.

Also on May 15, 2020, *NBC News* "fact-checked" the President's claim that "he thinks we're going to have a vaccine by the end of the year," stating "*Experts say he needs a 'miracle' to be right.*" See *nbcnews.com*:

Fact check: Coronavirus vaccine could come this year, Trump says. Experts say he needs a 'miracle' to be right.

When President Trump again made the claim, at the Republican National Convention in August 2020, that a vaccine would be available before the end of the year, *NBC News* again "fact checked" the statement, claiming the President's claim was "largely false," stating, among other things, that "There is also no evidence that an effective vaccine will be delivered by the end of the year." See *NBC News*, "*Updates and analysis from Day 4 of the Republican National Convention; Fact check: No evidence for Trump's COVID-19 vaccine claim*," August 27, 2020, *nbcnews.com*.

Barron's was also openly skeptical of the President's claim, made in August 2020, that a vaccine will be ready before the of 2020. See *"President Trump Promised a Vaccine Before the End of the Year. What You Need to Know,"* August 28, 2020, *barrons.com.* The article questions whether the vaccines could complete the clinical trials and be approved in time to meet the President's suggested timeline.

When President Trump claimed, in September 2020, a vaccine could be ready and in distribution before the end of the year, news outlets questioned the claim casting doubt on its validity. See *Global News, "Trump contradicts health officials, claims coronavirus vaccine could be ready next month,"* September 16, 2020, *globalnews.ca* and *Bloomberg, "Trump rebuts Doctors, Says Vaccine to Be Given Widely in October,"* September 16, 2020, *Bloomberg.com.*

On October 29, 2020, *Yahoo News* published an article entitled, *"Trump's vaccine promises meet reality,"* throwing cold water on the President's claims that a vaccine would be ready by the end of the year. See *yahoo.com.*

THE TRUTH

President Trump was right again.

Both the Pfizer-BioNTech mRNA COVID-19 vaccine and the Moderna mRNA COVID-19 vaccine completed their abbreviated Phase 3 trials and began being distributed before the end of the calendar year 2020. See *Pfizer Press Release*, November 9, 2020 and *BBC, "Moderna: Covid vaccine shows nearly 95% protection,"* November 16, 2020, *bbc.com.*

 The Pfizer-BioNTech mRNA COVID-19 vaccine was granted Emergency Use Authorization by the FDA on December 11, 2020. See *American Journal of Managed Care*, December 11, 2020, *ajmc.com*:

FDA Agrees to EUA for COVID-19 Vaccine From Pfizer, BioNTech

The Moderna mRNA COVID-19 vaccine received its Emergency Use Authoriza-tion from the FDA one week later on December 18, 2020. See *FDA*, December 18, 2020, *fda.gov*:

FDA Takes Additional Action in Fight Against COVID-19 By Issuing Emergency Use Authorization for Second COVID-19 Vaccine

The Johnson & Johnson vaccine received its Emergency Use Authorization from the FDA on February 27, 2020. See *American Journal of Managed Care*, December 11, 2020, *ajmc.com*:

A Timeline of COVID-19 Vaccine Developments in 2021

The two most widely available and widely distributed COVID-19 vaccines in the world were both approved and being administered to the American populace BEFORE the end of the calendar year 2020.

<u>Commentary</u>: President Trump repeatedly expressed his belief in 2020 that a COVID-19 vaccine would be approved and distributed to the American people before the end of the calendar year 2020. The Fake News Media had to question those claims simply because of the political implications. If President Trump were right, Joe Biden's chances of winning the Presidential Election dropped precipitously. Lo and behold, only six days after Election Day on November 3, 2020, Pfizer announced, on November 9, 2020, the results of its abbreviated Phase 3 trials. How about that? Are you wondering if that announcement

could have been made 7 or 8 days earlier, in time to prove President Trump was right BEFORE Election Day ? If you wonder about that, well, so do I. (That is yet another investigation and another story for another time.)

For my part, I believe *Operation Warp Speed*, the accelerated COVID-19 vaccine development program, was a colossal mistake. The people of this Country, indeed of the entire world, will likely deal with the health fall-out from these vaccines for many years to come. But the fact of the matter is President Trump and his Administration put together the unprecedented collaboration of industry and government to develop these vaccines and cleared the regulatory obstacles out of the way to allow the process to move forward with incredible speed. President Trump was in regular contact with the key players. When he said the vaccines were coming by the end of the year, he knew what he was talking about. He was right. The Fake News Media was wrong. As one op-ed piece in the *Wall Street Journal* questioned on November 18, 2020, "*Do media 'fact checkers' owe the President an apology?*" *wsj.com*. Yes, they do. But, don't hold your breath waiting for it.

5

TRUMP THREATENS DEMOCRACY BY REFUSING TO ACCEPT THE ELECTION RESULTS

But when Hillary Clinton refuses to accept election results, that is Democracy in Action!

THE FAKE NEWS

President Trump's unwillingness to accept the results of, and legal challenges to, the 2020 election were dangerous and a threat to our Democracy.

Who Pushed the Fake News?

The usual suspects were at work again. Former President Barack Obama claimed President Trump's refusal to accept the results of the 2020 Presidential election was a "dangerous path" and was "delegitimizing" democracy in America.See *Politico*, November 12, 2020, *politico.com*:

Obama: Trump's refusal to accept defeat is a 'dangerous path' for democracy

The former president also stated, Trump's refusal to accept the results was ". . . one more step in delegitimizing not just the incoming Biden administration, but democracy in general." See also, *USA Today*, November 13, 2020, *usatoday.com*:

Obama says he's 'troubled' Republicans are backing Trump in his refusal to concede to Biden

Cindy McCain, the wife of the late U.S. Senator John McCain was quoted in the same article claiming, with respect to President Trump's unwillingness to accept defeat, "It's dangerous for this to occur." See *Politico*, "*Obama: Trump's refusal to accept defeat is a 'dangerous path' for democracy*," November 12, 2020, *politico.com*.

Transforming Society claimed, in article posted online on November 18, 2020, that President Trump's refusal to concede "is a major threat" to "democracy." See *transformingsociety.co.uk*:

Donald Trump's refusal to concede is a major threat to US democracy

An opinion article in *Business Insider* claimed President Trump's refusal to concede the election undermines "America's democratic message abroad and emboldens dictators and authoritarians.," in an article published on November 18, 2020. See *"Trump's refusal to concede not only hurts America's democratic message abroad, it also gives a useful tool to the world's authoritarians,"* November 18, 2020, *businessinsider.com.*

Time Magazine called President Trump's legal challenges "A long-shot strategy with lasting damage to American democracy" in an article published on November 19, 2020. See *"People Will Stop Believing in the Process. Why Donald Trump's Legal Strategy is Dangerous Even If It's Likely to Fail,"* November 18, 2020, *time.com.*

The Economist claimed President Trump's refusal to concede the election was "harming America" in an article published on November 21, 2020. See *"Donald Trump's refusal to concede is harming America,"* *economist.com.*

The New York Times claimed President Trump was trying to "undo" an election result and posed a "one of the gravest threats to our democracy" in an article published on November 12, 2020. See *"Good morning. A president is trying to undo an election result: How would you describe that situation in another country?"* November 12, 2020, *nytimes.com.*

On November 20, 2020, *PBS News Hour* hosted syndicated columnist Mark Shields and *New York Times* columnist David Brooks who railed about how "reprehensible" President Trump's challenges to the election were and how he and Republican supporters were "undoing democracy." See *"Sheilds and Brooks on the danger of Trump's refusal to concede,"* November 20, 2020, *pbs.org.*

There are literally dozens of articles, reports and broadcasts claiming President Trump's refusal to "accept" the results of the election or concede to Joe Biden or his legal challenges to the election or his unwillingness to cooperate during the early phases of the transition were damaging our democracy, were "anti" democratic, "dangerous," would undermine the legitimacy of the Biden Presidency, would embolden foreign dictators, etc...

THE TRUTH

If challenging election results might "delegitimize" an incoming president and our Country, how about high-ranking, prominent elected officials and Democrat Party officials outright claiming a president is illegitimate like the Democrats did after Donald Trump won in 2016? What did the media say about that?

If challenging election results or refusing to concede an election were a "danger" to our Republic or if refusing to acknowledge the results would delegitimize the winner's office, what did Fake News Media say in 2016 when Green Party candidate Jill Stein and Democrat Party nominee Hillary Clinton challenged the 2016 election results? And what did the Fake News Media say about the refusal of Democrats to "accept" President Trump's win? Let us take a look.

As *The Washington Times* reported on January 16, 2017, in an article entitled, *"Jerry Nadler: Trump election 'illegitimate,' won't attend inauguration,"* the paper noted that "dozens" of Democrats in the United States House of Representatives planned to skip Donald Trump's inauguration. Rep. Jerrold Nadler (D-NY) said Donald Trump's election was "illegitimate" due to the FBI "weighing-in on the election." Rep. Steven Cohen (D-Tenn) was quoted in the article calling Donald Trump the "president semi-elect." See *washingtontimes.com.*

In an article published on January 13, 2017, *NBC News* quoted Democrat U.S. Rep. John Lewis (D-GA) in the article's title, *"Rep. John Lewis: 'I Don't See Trump as a Legitimate President,"* adding in the sub-title, that Rep. Lewis believes " . . . the Russians participated in helping this man get elected." Missing from the article is any criticism or condemnation of Rep. Lewis:

Rep. John Lewis: 'I Don't See Trump as a Legitimate President'

Former Democrat President Jimmy Carter also claimed President Trump was not a legitimate president in statements made on June 28, 2019. See *CNN, cnn.com*:

Jimmy Carter suggests Trump is an illegitimate president

In a campaign stop in May 2019, then candidate Joe Biden said he "absolutely agreed" with a lady who claimed President Trump was "illegitimate" and might get elected again with the "help of Vlad, his best pal." See *Fox News*, "*Biden 'absolutely' agrees with woman who blasts Trump presidency by calling it 'illegitimate.*" May 14, 2019, *foxnews.com*.

Hillary Clinton claimed President Trump was an "illegitimate president" because of "voter suppression and voter purging to hacking to the false stories." See *Fox News*, "*Hillary Clinton calls Trump 'illegitimate president' and 'corrupt human tornado,*" September 26, 2019, *foxnews.com* (Listening to Hillary Clinton call someone else "corrupt" is painful indeed.)

Hillary Clinton calls Trump 'illegitimate president' and 'corrupt human tornado'

See also, *The Washington Post*, "*Hillary Clinton: Trump is an 'illegitimate president,*" September 26, 2019, *washingtonpost.com*.

What happened after all of the Fake News Media and Democrat propaganda about Donald Trump being an "illegitimate" president? At least one survey showed a majority of young Americans viewed Donald Trump's presidency as "illegitimate." See *NBC News, "Majority of Young Americans View Trump as Illegitimate President: Poll,"* March 19, 2017, *nbcnews.com.* (Some in the Fake News Media probably read this and thought "mission accomplished.")

The Guardian published a story on November 8, 2017 entitled, *"One year on, Donald Trump is still an illegitimate president."* See *theguardian.com.* This article reads like a dime store piece of comic book fiction, if you are able to stomach reading it. So much for delegitimizing a sitting president being "dangerous" to Democracy:

One year on, Donald Trump is still an illegitimate president

Maclean's literally published an entire article on January 18, 2017, about how Democrats were challenging Donald Trump's legitimacy and how that might be a more effective tactic than attacking his character. The article is entitled, *"Why calling Trump illegitimate might legitimately work,"* and literally states, "By implying he was installed by forces hostile to the U.S., or that the election was tainted by interference from the FBI, they plant the notion in people's heads that he won't deliver on what he's promising." The piece further declared, ". . . delegitimizing a president can work by creating suspicion of him, even among people who don't dislike him personally." See *macleans.ca.*

The New York Intelligencer published an article on November 22, 2016, entitled, *"Experts Urge Clinton Campaign to Challenge Election Results in 3 Swing States,"* claiming a group of "prominent computer scientists and election lawyers" called for the Clinton Campaign to demand a recount and audits in Wisconsin, Michigan and Pennsylvania due to "persuasive evidence" the results in those states in 2016 were "manipulated or hacked." These experts called for the audit of election machines as part of the challenge. Not one word about "threats to Democracy" or "dangerousness" or "undermining the legitimacy" of Trump's Presidency from the magazine. See *nymag.com*:

Experts Urge Clinton Campaign to Challenge Election Results in 3 Swing States

Readers may recall, after the 2016 election, Green Party candidate Dr. Jill Stein requested recounts in multiple states, including Wisconsin. The Clinton campaign joined her efforts. Review some of the media reports about the Stein/Clinton recounts.

NBC News reported on the Clinton campaign backing Jill Stein's Wisconsin recount on November 26, 2020, in an article entitled, *"Clinton Campaign Backs Jill Stein's Election Recount Effort: Lawyer."* What is missing from the report? Any mention that challenging the results is "dangerous" or threatens to "undermine" or "delegitimize" the incoming Trump Administration. The article is replete with multiple quotes from Clinton campaign attorneys claiming they must ensure the process is "fair to all sides" and ". . . it is a fundamental principle of our democracy to ensure that every vote is properly counted." Nice. (See *nbcnews.com*.)

National Public Radio published a similar piece on the same day, November 26, 2020, noting the Clinton campaign would participate in the recount. The article quotes Green Party candidate Jill Stein who stated her challenge was made to ensure elections in the United States are "fair and reliable" and that "We need a system that empowers voters, and that needs to start with a voting system we can trust." (Implicit in this statement is the notion that the

American voting system cannot be trusted, right? But, not a word about that or any critical word about the Stein/Clinton campaign's efforts.) See *NPR*, *"Clinton Campaign Says It Will Participate In Recount Efforts,"* November 26, 2016, *npr.org*.

As *The Guardian* reported on November 23, 2016, *"Hillary Clinton urged to call for election vote recount in battleground states."* The article outlines the need for an election audit due to concerns over 'foreign hackers." See *theguardian.com*.

After Hillary Clinton lost the Presidential Election in 2016, some in the media went on and on about the vulnerability of American elections and election systems.

Politico reported *"U.S. elections are more vulnerable than ever to hacking,"* in an article published December 29, 2019. In the article, *Politico* elaborated on the "massive, flawed election process," due to a lack of cyber protections. See *politico.com*.

In another article *Politico* published on August 5, 2016, computer science experts showed how to compromise antiquated voting machines literally in minutes. The article entitled, *"How to Hack an Election in 7 Minutes,"* goes on to outline various different election vulnerabilities around the Country, how various different voting machines are subject to easily being compromised, how unprepared American States, counties and election clerks are for cyber attacks and generally outlining the susceptibility of our voting systems to being manipulated and, thereby, manipulating elections. See *politico.com*.

In an article published on November 23, 2016, *WIRED* proclaimed, *"Hacked or not, Audit This Election (And All Future Ones),"* *wired.com*, and outlined some of the issues with electronic voting machines in the United States and the need for regular audits due to the vulnerability of voting systems to hacks:

Hacked or Not, Audit This Election (And All Future Ones)

In an earlier article entitled, *"America's Electronic Voting Machines Are Scarily Easy Targets,"* on August 2, 2016, *wired.com* outlined some of the actual vulnerabilities in American electronic voting systems and how easily bad actors could manipulate our elections.

The Intercept reported on October 3, 2017, that *"The U.S. Election System Remains Deeply Vulnerable, But States Would Rather Celebrate Fake Success,"* outlining the susceptibility of voter registrations systems and voting software across the Country (even providing some illustrations of systems being hacked or tampered with) and the need to secure them. See *theintercept.com*.

If failing to concede the election "threatens our democracy," then Hillary Clinton threatened our democracy yet again a couple of months before the 2020 Presidential Election when she advised the Democrat nominee, Joe Biden to NOT concede the election "under any circumstances." See *NBC News, "Hillary Clinton says Biden should not concede the election 'under any circumstances,"* August 26, 2020, *nbcnews.com.* Yet, despite this proclamation, Hillary Clinton was not criticized at all by Fake News Media.

Clearly, when Democrats question the vulnerability of election systems and question the validity of an election, our democracy is not challenged or "threatened" at all. Rather, the Fake News Media spins it all as democracy at work.

Commentary: Articles, reports and broadcasts similar to those cited above could be cited endlessly, but the point is made. Democrats literally called President Trump an illegitimate president for years, but the Fake News Media does not claim those efforts undermine our democracy and does not call out anyone for undermining Donald Trump and his Administration (undermining Trump was their intent after all, right?). A number of good articles were written about the Democrat attacks on the legitimacy of Donald Trump's presidency for those interested in further reading on the subject. See *The Federalist*, "*Democrats Have Been Denying Trump The Presidency Ever Since His First Victory*," November 5, 2020, *the federalist.com*, *The Washington Examiner*, "*Byron York's Daily Memo: A New York Times embarrassment*," December 1, 2020, *washingtonexaminer.com*, and *The New York Post*, "*Yes, Democrats denied Trump's legitimacy and other commentary*," December 6, 2020, *nypost.com*, for starters.

A review of the articles and reports about the Democrats' claims that Trump's presidency was "illegitimate" reflects the basis for the claims was overwhelmingly phony "Russia collusion." Of course, the entire "Russia collusion" narrative was complete, utter rubbish and Fake News. Donald Trump and his campaign did not "collude" with the Russians at all. Furthermore, we now know the "Russia collusion" narrative was concocted by the Clinton campaign and Democrat Party initially to try to help Clinton win the 2016 election and, later used to undermine President Trump and his Administration. (All of these issues are delved into deeply in Volumes Two and Three of this book series.) The fact so many Democrat politicians and Party leaders used this Clinton Campaign and Democrat Party concocted hogwash for years to attack Donald Trump and the legitimacy of his Presidency is unconscionable.

When a third-party candidate, Hillary Clinton or others call into question the accuracy of election results, demand recounts, demand election audits or call into question the potential for voting systems to be hacked, they are not derided by the Fake News Media as undermining our democracy, delegitimizing our democracy or the presidency. In fact, the Fake News Media does not attack the Democrats when they openly delegitimized the Trump Presidency. In the eyes of the Fake News Media only *Donald Trump's* challenges to the integrity of our voting systems or his reluctance to concede an election "threaten" our democracy. (As I will outline in an upcoming book, Fake News Media cheer leads when *Democrats* actually threaten our democracy, such as the effort to promote "faithless electors" in the Electoral College in 2016 to deny Donald

Trump the Presidency. See *Politico*, "*Democratic presidential electors revolt against Trump*," November 22, 2016, *politico.com*.) Keep this in mind the next time the Fake News Media claims a Republican is "threatening" our form of government.

6

THE FIRST LADY BROKE HOSPITAL RULES BY READING TO CHILDREN WITHOUT HER MASK?

No, First Lady Melania Trump violated no rules at all.

THE FAKE NEWS

The First Lady, Melania Trump, violated the masking policy at Children's National Hospital on December 15, 2020, when she removed her mask to read a holiday book to children.

Who Pushed the Fake News?

CNN lead the charge with an article published on December 15, 2020, entitled, *"Melania Trump breaks children's hospital rules by taking her mask off to read to patients,"* cnn.com:

Melania Trump breaks children's hospital rules by taking her mask off to read to patients

The article details how the First Lady visited children at the hospital each year during President Trump's term, but criticized her for continuing the tradition ". . . despite the coronavirus pandemic and record cases in Washington, DC." Only a few children were present for the reading, but the reading was broadcast to all of the patient rooms.

The article claimed the hospital policy requires "everyone to wear a mask at all times" while in the facility and that the First Lady, despite maintaining social distancing from anyone else present, violated the policy by removing her mask to read.

The Hill ran with the story originally entitled, "*Melania Trump removes mask to read to young patients, breaking hospital's rules,*" December 15, 2020, thehill.com. The article stated, in part, "First lady Melanie Trump took off her mask on Tuesday to read to children at the Children's National Hospital, where hospital policy requires visitors to wear a face covering though officials noted she sat away from others." *The Hill* article includes video of the First Lady entering the room with her mask on, sitting in front of a Christmas tree and removing her mask while she sits by herself in a chair.

The Economic Times version of the story is entitled, "*Melanie Trump puts children at risk as she takes off her mask during a reading,*" December 16, 2020, economictimes.indiatimes.com:

Melania Trump puts children at risk as she takes off her mask during a reading

Despite the ridiculous title of the story, this piece contains several photographs not found in the other stories. These photographs show how far away the First Lady was from the few people in the room when she removed her mask.

THE TRUTH

The First Lady did not violate Children's National Hospital policy when she removed her mask to read to the children. She was in compliance with the policy. She certainly did not place any children at risk of anything, as the First Lady was more than 12 feet away from the only two children in the room (the rest watched by closed circuit TV).

The policy relied upon by CNN to claim the First Lady was in violation was posted on the hospital's website. After the story was published, Children's National Hospital released the following statement:

Our number one priority at Children's National Hospital is the safety of our patients, families and employees.

The hospital website does not include the mask policy for people who come to the hospital to give a speech. The First Lady did follow our mask protocols for public speakers, which is based on DC Health Guidance, which states that wearing a mask is not required when a person is giving a speech for broadcast or an audience provided no one is within six feet of the speaker.

In the case of today's visit, which was broadcast to our patient's rooms, when the First Lady did remove her mask while she read a story, she was more than twelve feet away from others in our four-story atrium. This space was closed off from hospital visitors and the small group of people in that space were wearing all wearing masks. (sic) For the remainder of the First Lady's visit, she wore a mask and did not visit any patient care areas.

See *The Right Scoop,* "*CNN smears Melania Trump for taking off her mask at hospital, then REFUSES to correct misreporting when proven WRONG,*" December

15, 2020, *therightscoop.com* and *Mediaite*, December 16, 2020, *mediaite.com*:

CNN, *The Hill* Fail to Correct False Story Claiming Melania Trump Violated Children's Hospital Mask Policy

What did the Fake News Media do once they were confronted with the truth?

Well, *CNN* refused to alter its headline and persisted with the false claim the First Lady violated hospital rules. This fact is addressed directly in *The Right Scoop* article cited above. *CNN* added an italicized statement at the end of the article reflecting *"This story has been updated with comments from the White House readout of the event."*

The Hill changed its original headline from *"Melania Trump removes mask to read to young patients, breaking hospital's rules"* to *"Melanie Trump removes mask to read to young patients at hospital."* The *Mediaite* article cited above actually contains both headlines to document the change.

Commentary: No First Lady in modern times received worse treatment from the media than Melania Trump. Despite being a beautiful, sophisticated, highly educated, multi-lingual, successful immigrant, she was repeatedly attacked and maligned. She brought grace, style, beauty, professionalism and thoughtfulness to the White House. Melania Trump should have been promoted and idolized as a role model for young American women and recent young immigrants to the USA, in particular. Instead, the Fake News Media rarely missed an opportunity to disparage her. This story about reading to the children is a good illustration. The First Lady did not violate any hospital policy by sitting in a giant room, more than 12 feet away from people, and removing her mask to read to children (all but two of whom watched by closed circuit TV). She certainly did not place any children at risk of catching coronavirus (or anything else) since she was more than 12 feet away (twice the distance recommended by DC Health Guidance) from the only two children in the room while the rest watched on closed circuit TV.

Ask yourself this, would this story have seen the light of day if former First Lady Michelle Obama was the one doing the reading? Of course, not. Had former First Lady Obama been the one reading the story the headlines would have read something along these lines, *"First Lady visits sick kids at Children's National Hospital and raises their spirits by reading a lively Christmas story while exceeding COVID social distancing requirements."* Instead, you see the treatment Melania Trump received.

Could you imagine the outrage in the Fake News Media if a staffer surreptitiously recorded Michelle Obama the way Stephanie Winston Wolkoff recorded Melania Trump? (See *CNN*, *"Secretly recorded tapes show Melania Trump's frustration at criticism for family separation policy and her bashing of Christmas decorations,"* October 2, 2020, *cnn.com.*) Would any Fake News Media outlet even publish such a recording of Michelle Obama? (Certainly, no outlet would publish it with the glee that *CNN* did the Melania Trump tape.)

The Hill published a nice opinion piece about former First Lady Melania Trump on January 21, 2021, entitled, *"Scorned and mistreated, Melania Trump deserved much better from the media,"* thehill.com. The article outlines some of the disgraceful attacks on First Lady Melania Trump and ends with the observation that she ". . . deserved much, much better."

Scorned and mistreated, Melania Trump deserved much better from the media

You can say that again.

7

CAPITOL POLICE OFFICER DIES FROM HEAD TRAUMA SUSTAINED IN JAN. 6 RIOT?

No, his untimely death was from natural causes.

<u>Background</u>: The next few chapters deal with the pro-Trump protests which took place on January 6, 2021. These protests are commonly referred to in media reports as the "Capitol Riot," though the original protests did not take place at the Capitol Buildings and only a tiny fraction of the crowd had anything to do with the rioting. Much of what you read and heard about the events of January 6, 2021 is bombastic hyperbole or misinformation. An entire book could be written about these issues, however, that is for another time. The next few chapters will outline some of the most basic forms of Fake News circulated about January 6. Some background information is needed, however, to put the events into context.

The short version on background is this: January 6, 2021 was the date the U.S. House and Senate met in a Joint Session to certify the results from the Electoral College and, thereby, certify the results of the 2020 Presidential Election. That is why the "Save America" rallies were originally scheduled by

Trump supporters on this day, to try to demonstrate the numbers of people concerned about the 2020 election results and support efforts to challenge the certification of the vote by Congress. (The official permit issued by The United States Department of the Interior, National Park Service for the public gathering reflect multiple events over several days.)

For those readers interested in more background and context, read on. First of all, as the readers of this book are undoubtedly aware, President Trump, some other Republican officials and millions of Trump supporters and concerned citizens believed (and continue to believe) the November 3, 2020, Presidential Election was "stolen" or "rigged" through a series of abuses involving private funding (by leftist billionaires) of Democrat-controlled urban elections offices in swing states, abuses of mail in ballots ostensibly needed due to the Coronavirus pandemic, the use of illegal "ballot harvesting" operations in swing states and more. (The nature, extent and effect of these operations and the 2020 Presidential Election generally are the subject of another book I am working on and are beyond the scope of this book. Suffice it to say, however, many of the claims of President Trump, other elected officials and the concerns of millions of Trump supporters and other Americans were, and are, well-founded.)

What do the election manipulations have to do with January 6, 2021? To understand that, background is needed on how the President is elected in the United States. When Americans go to the polls on Election Day to vote for President they are actually voting in each State for a slate of "electors." The slates of electors are pledged to vote for a particular candidate. Each State is assigned a number of electors corresponding to the number of Congressional Representatives the State has (remember, Congressional seats are apportioned based on population), plus two for the State's United States Senators (in addition the District of Columbia gets three electors). There are a total of 435 house seats, 100 senate seats and 3 electors for the District of Columbia, bringing the total number of electors to 538. Each State's slate of electors then meets in their respective State Capitols in mid-

December and cast their votes. Under Federal law, on the January 6 following each Presidential Election, the States' electoral votes are officially opened and counted in a Joint Session of Congress in the United States House of Representatives with the Vice President presiding. A candidate must receive 270 of the 538 electoral votes to become President or Vice President. A good description of the process is provided by *The National Archives*, *"Choosing a President: How the Electoral College Works,"* archives.gov.

Thus, January 6, 2021, was the day the Joint Session of the United States Congress convened in the United States House of Representatives with the Vice President Mike Pence presiding. Various different pro-Trump politicians, business people, activists and others organized a rally for January 6, 2021, called the "Save America Rally." President Trump, former New York City Mayor Rudy Giuliani, attorney and law professor John Eastman, U.S. Rep. Madison Cawthorn and U.S. Rep. Mo Brooks, among others spoke at the rally. Basically, the President and the other speakers at the rally wanted the Vice President to refuse to accept the certification and send the slates of electors from the challenged swing States back to those States to recertify and/or have Congress vote against certifying the election. The transcript of President Trump's speech reflects this (the transcript may be found at *kiiitv.com*), as does video of the speech of law professor John Eastman, confirming the point is to have Vice President Pence "let the legislatures of the States look into this" at 8:05 to 8:15 of the video (the video may be found at *c-span.org*).

The Save the America Rally where President Trump (and Mayor Giuliani and the others) made their speeches was at the Ellipse near the White House. Many of the people attending the Save America Rally left and went to the Capitol grounds. Estimates on the number of people on the Capitol grounds are in the range of 10,000 with somewhere between 1,000 and 2,500 entering the Capitol Buildings. (See Capitol Police Chief estimate, *ABC Columbia*, *"Acting Capitol Police Chief: Nearly 1,000 people breached the Capitol on January 6,"* February 25, 2021, abccolumbia.com and *ABC News*, *"By the numbers: How the Jan. 6 investigation is shaping up 1 year later,"* January 4, 2022, abcnews.go.com, though early estimates immediately after the events put the number of people who breached the Capitol Buildings at under 1,000. See *Buzz Feed News,* *"Hundreds Of People Who Joined the Capitol Riot May Never Face Charges,"* March 16, 2021, *buzzfeednews.com.*)

The Democrats in Washington, D.C., and the Fake News Media deliberately hyped the events to justify the second impeachment of President Trump. Some of the hyperbolic nonsense is addressed in this chapter and several following chapters.

The facts which expose the J6 Committee as a pure propaganda ploy is the person the Democrats selected to chair it, Mississippi Democrat Congressman Bennie Thompson. Congressman Thompson is a long-time sympathizer of the Republic of New Afrika and some of its membership. See *Just the News,* *"Jan. 6 commission chairman once sympathized with black secessionist group that killed cops,"* October 4, 2021, *justthenews.com.* For the uninitiated, the Republic of New Afrika (RNA) is a revolutionary, militant black organization formed in 1968. See *blackpast.org, "Republic of New Africa,"* March 10, 2012. One of the goals of this revolutionary organization is the establishment of an independent "New Afrika" nation consisting of the states of Louisiana, Mississippi, Alabama, Georgia and South Carolina. Various leaders and members of the organization were involved in shootouts with police and the FBI over the years. Some of these episodes are outlined in the article by John Solomon cited above.

Rep. Thompson's affiliations with RNA began when he was an Alderman in Bolton, Mississippi back in 1971 when he publicly attacked police after some RNA members were arrested. As recently as 2013, when the former Vice President of the Republic of New Afrika, Chokwe Lumumba, ran for Mayor of the City of Jackson, Mississippi, Congressman Thompson supported him. See *Jackson Free Press, "Bennie Thompson Backs Lumumba, Links Lee to GOP,"* May 17, 2013, *jacksonfreepress.com.* In fact, Rep. Thompson participated in campaign ads supporting Lumumba. When the revolutionary black militant won the Jackson Mayor's race, Rep. Thompson officiated at his induction ceremony. See *Just the News*, "*Jan. 6 commission chairman once sympathized with black secessionist group that killed cops*," October 4, 2021, *justthenews.com*.

This is the guy the Democrats put in charge of investigating an alleged "insurrection?" A man linked to a radical, revolutionary, black militant group that wants to declare a new homeland in five U.S. states? A group with a history of violent shootouts with law enforcement? That tells the world just how serious Democrats are about this so-called "insurrection." You could not make this lunacy up if you tried.

THE FAKE NEWS

Capitol Police Officer Brian Sicknick died on January 7 of injuries sustained during the January 6 Capitol riot when he was bludgeoned with a fire extinquisher.

Who Pushed the Fake News?

The New York Times ran with this story in an article entitled, "*Capitol Police Officer Dies from Injuries in Pro-Trump Rampage*," originally published on January 8, 2021. See *nytimes.com*:

Capitol Police Officer Dies From Injuries in Pro-Trump Rampage

In the story, the NYT cited two anonymous "law enforcement officials" as the source for the claim Officer Sicknick was "struck with a fire extinguisher" during the Capitol riot.

Also on January 8, 2021, *The New York Times* published, *"He Dreamed of Being a Police Officer Then Was Killed by a Pro-Trump Mob."* See *nytimes.com*. In the article, the story that Officer Sicknick was struck in the "head with a fire extinguisher" was repeated, again citing "two law enforcement officials." This time, the story is elaborated on and claims Officer Sicknick was "rushed to the hospital" with a "bloody gash in his head" and was "placed on life support." The NYT then uses the death of Officer Sicknick to claim President Trump used "law and order" to galvanize political support rather than help police.

Many other news outlets ran with some version of the story, including *The Wall Street Journal*, *"Capitol Police Officer Brian Sicknick Dies of Injuries Sustained in the Riot,"* January 8, 2021, *wsj.com*, *Reuters*, *"Homicide Investigation opened into death of Capitol Police officer,"* *web.archive.org*, and *The Associated Press*, January 8, 2021, *chicagotribune.com*:

Capitol Police Officer Dies From Injuries in Pro-Trump Rampage

The Capitol Police issued a statement after Officer Sicknick's death indicating he "passed away from injuries sustained while on duty" and that he "responded to the riots on Wednesday, January 6, 2021, at the U.S. Capitol and was injured while physically engaging with protestors." See *National Public Radio*, *"Police Confirm Death of Officer Injured During Attack on Capitol,"* January 7, 2021, *npr.com*.

In addition, the United States Department of Justice, Office of Public Affairs, issued a statement from Acting Attorney General Jeffrey A. Rosen offering his condolences to the family of Officer Sicknick and stating Officer Sicknick "succumbed to the injuries he suffered defending the U.S. Capitol, against the violent mob who stormed it on January 6th." See *justice.gov*, Friday, January

8, 2021.

The Fake News Media might be excused for falsely reporting Officer Sicknick's death was related to the January 6th protests given the statements issued by The Capitol Police and the Acting United States Attorney General. But, Fake News Media cannot refrain from digging up an anonymous source or two and adding some spice to any story they can.

Two individuals were ultimately arrested and charged for spraying Officer Sicknick with what was originally claimed to be bear spray. See *The Washington Post*, "*Two arrested in assault on police officer Brian D. Sicknick, who died after Jan. 6 Capitol riot*," March 15, 2021, *washingtonpost.com*. Though in a court hearing in April, the DOJ confirmed the officers were sprayed with pepper spray, not bear spray. See *CNN*, "*US Capitol rioters charged in Sicknick case were armed with bear spray but only used pepper spray, prosecutors say*," April 27, 2021, *web.archive.org*.

THE TRUTH

Capitol Police Officer Brian Sicknick's autopsy revealed he died of natural causes. Specifically, the D.C. Medical Examiner found Officer Sicknick died of two strokes caused by a blood clot at the base of his brain stem. The autopsy of Officer Sicknick revealed no physical injuries. He was not hit in the head with a fire extinguisher (or anything else) on January 6.

In an interview with *The Washington Post*, reported on April 19, 2021, the D.C. Medical Examiner, Francizco Diaz, confirmed Officer Sicknick died of natural causes. The autopsy found "no evidence" the officer suffered any "allergic reaction to chemical irritants" (referencing the pepper spray Officer Sicknick was sprayed with) and "no evidence of internal or external injuries." See *washingtonpost.com*:

Capitol Police officer Brian Sicknick, who engaged rioters, suffered two strokes and died of natural causes, officials say

The Medical Examiner also issued a time line for events leading up to Officer Sicknick's death.The Medical Examiner stated Officer Sicknick collapsed "seven hours and 40 minutes after he was sprayed and then died 24 hours after that." See *Times News*, "*At last we know the truth about officer's death,*" April 25, 2021, *timesnews.com*. (This is also reported in the original *Washington Post* story, cited above.)

Commentary: Capitol Police Officer Brian Sicknick was a young man, only 42 years old, at the time of his death. His death was untimely, and tragic, without any doubt. Furthermore, he should not have been called upon to deal with an unruly mob on January 6 and should not have been sprayed with pepper spray either. Nevertheless, nothing justifies the hyperbole and misinformation spewed by Government and Fake News Media sources after his death in their effort to elevate the events of January 6, 2021, into something they were not. The Fake News Media seeks to cast the events of January 6, 2021, as an "armed rebellion," or an attempt to overthrow the government and a grave threat to our Country, regardless of the ridiculousness of their contentions. Manipulating the facts and circumstances surrounding the untimely death of Officer Sicknick served their purposes.

8

TRUMP INCITED VIOLENCE IN HIS JAN. 6 SPEECH

No, he did not.

THE FAKE NEWS

President Trump incited violence and insurrection at his speech at the Save America Rally on January 6, 2021.

Who Pushed the Fake News?

The Fake News Media conjured this narrative almost immediately. The stories started popping up the same day, January 6, 2021, claiming President Trump incited violence. One of the first was the *Los Angeles Times* with its article, *"Long warned against inciting violence, Trump does so with supporters' Capitol siege," latimes.com*:

Long warned against inciting violence, Trump does so with supporters' Capitol siege

By the next day, January 7, 2020, Nancy Pelosi, Democrat and Speaker of the United States House of Representatives publicly claimed that President Trump "incited" an "insurrection" the previous day. See *"Nancy Pelosi Press Conference on Capitol Riot, 25th Amendment Transcript, January 7,"* January 7, 2021, *rev.com*.

The Democrat-controlled United States House of Representatives pushed this precise Fake News in their *Articles of Impeachment* passed on January 25, 2021.

The *Articles of Impeachment* selectively quotes fourteen words from President Trump's speech, namely, the quote, ". . . if you don't fight like hell you're not going to have a country anymore," coupled with President Trump's claim that he actually won the election (which he, in all probability, actually did) as inciting violence and insurrection. See *Congress.gov*.

One media outlet after another made the same claim.

VOX ran the story on January 8, 2021, with an article *"How Trump's speech led to the Capitol riot,"* *vox.com*.

Time Magazine published a story on the topic entitled, *"Incited by President, Trump Supporters Storm the Capitol,"* January 7, 2021, *time.com*:

Incited by the President, Pro-Trump Rioters Violently Storm the Capitol

Buzz Feed News led the charge with an article entitled, *"Trump Launched A Deadly Attempted Coup, Encouraging A Mob To Breach The US Capitol Building Because He Lost The Presidential Election,"* January 7, 2021, *buzzfeednews.com*:

Trump Launched A Deadly Attempted Coup, Encouraging A Mob To Breach The US Capitol Building Because He Lost The Presidential Election

Fortune ran the claim with "*'We will never concede': How Donald Trump incited an attack on America,*" on January 7, 2021, *fortune.com*.

Central to all, or virtually all, of these claims are the "fight like hell" quote, cited above, as well as President Trump's claims the 2020 Presidential Election was stolen by Biden and the Democrat Party and his claims that he actually won the election.

THE TRUTH

President Trump did not "incite" any violence or insurrection in his January 6, 2021 speech. All one needs to do is to watch and listen to the speech on video or read the transcript of it to confirm this fact. A video and transcript of the speech may be found here: https://www.npr.org/2021/02/10/9663968 48/read-trumps-jan-6-speech-a-key-part-of-impeachment-trial. (The President's remarks start at approximately the 41:00 minute mark.)

Keep in mind, as the previous Chapter outlined, a Joint Session of the United States House of Representatives and United States Senate would vote on certifying the results from the Electoral College later the afternoon of January 6, 2020, some time after President Trump's speech. President Trump hoped to get Vice President Mike Pence, who presided over the Joint Session, to reject slates of electors from the States contested by the Trump campaign or to have the Joint Session vote to not certify the results. President Trump's remarks were made in this context.

For convenience, some of President Trump's comments are reproduced below (with minute and second references to the video):

. . . and I hope Mike is going to do the right thing. I hope so. I hope so.

Because if Mike Pence does the right thing, we win the election. All he has to do, all this is, this is from the number one, or certainly one of the top, Constitutional lawyers in our country. He has the absolute right to do it. We're supposed to protect our country, support our country, support our Constitution, and protect our constitution.

States want to revote. The states got defrauded. They were given false information. They voted on it. Now they want to recertify. They want it back. All Vice President Pence has to do is send it back to the states to recertify and we become president and you are the happiest people.

(Video at 47:17.)

The next part of the speech reproduced here is the first reference to "fighting" in the speech. The statement is made in reference to electing Republicans who are not weak and who will challenge Democrats:

And you have to get your people to fight. And if they don't fight, we have to primary the hell out of the ones that don't fight. You primary them. We're going to. We're going to let you know who they are. I can already tell you, frankly.

(Video at 53:34.)

The next portion quoted is where President Trump speaks about what he and his supporters want Congress to do and about walking down to the Capitol after the rally:

Now, it is up to Congress to confront this egregious assault on our democracy. And after this, we're going to walk down, and I'll be there with you, we're going to walk down, we're going to walk down.

*Anyone you want, but I think right here, we're going to walk down to the Capitol, and **we're going to cheer on our brave senators and congressmen and women**, and we're probably not going to be cheering so much for some of them.*

Because you'll never take back our country with weakness. You have to show strength and you have to be strong. We have come to demand that Congress do the right thing and only count the electors who have been lawfully slated, lawfully slated.

*I know that everyone here will soon be marching over to the Capitol building **to peacefully and patriotically** make your voices heard.*

(Video at 56:39.)

After a lengthy discussion about election irregularities in various States, President Trump utters the words cited so selectively by the Fake News Media and Democrats (here the oft-quoted comments are provided with some surrounding comments for context):

We have overwhelming pride in this great country and we have it deep in our souls. Together, we are determined to defend and preserve government of the people, by the people and for the people.

Our brightest days are before us. Our greatest achievements, still away.

I think one of our great achievements will be election security. Because nobody until I came along had any idea how corrupt our elections were.

And again, most people would stand there at 9 o'clock in the evening and say I want to thank you very much, and they go off to some other life. But I said something's wrong here, something is really wrong, can have happened.

And we fight. We fight like hell. And if you don't fight like hell, you're not going to have a country anymore.

Our exciting adventures and boldest endeavors have not yet begun. My fellow Americans, for our movement, for our children, and for our beloved country.

(Video at 1:50:33.)

There is not a hint of, nor a mention of, violence or insurrection or rioting in the entire speech. None at all. Any contention to the contrary is complete, utter nonsense.

Furthermore, as most Americans are aware, the people of this Country enjoy Freedom of Speech under the First Amendment to the United States Constitution.The First Amendment is implicated here, because speech like President Trump's on January 6, 2021, cannot be criminalized even if the District of Columbia tried to criminalize it.

The Supreme Court set fort the test for what is known as "inflammatory speech" (though there is zero "inflammatory speech" in President Trump's speech of January 6, 2021) in *Brandenburg v. Ohio* in 1969. In that case, a Ku Klux Klansman in Ohio was prosecuted and convicted under an Ohio law for "advocating" for "crime, sabotage, violence or unlawful methods of terrorism," for racist speech and threats about taking "revengeance." The Supreme Court reversed the conviction finding the man's speech was protected by the First Amendment.

The Supreme Court fashioned a test for inflammatory speech finding the law may prohibit speech advocating use of force or crime if the speech:

1. Is "directed to inciting or producing imminent lawless action," AND
2. Is "likely to incite or produce such action."

See *https://www.law.cornell.edu/wex/brandenburg_test.* (Cornell Law School page listing the *Brandenburg* test).

Anyone can see President Trump's January 6, 2021, speech in no way met the *Brandenburg* test and, therefore, remained completely, totally protected by the First Amendment.

Additionally, the District of Columbia has two separate provisions of law which are arguably applicable to inciting riots. Review of those confirms, again, that President Trump did NOTHING in violation of these laws in his January 6 speech, even if the First Amendment to the United States Constitution did not exist to protect his speech.

Specifically, D.C. Code §22-1321, Disorderly Conduct, provides:

(A) In any place open to the public . . . it is unlawful to:

(1) intentionally or recklessly act in such a manner as to cause another person to be in reasonable fear that a person or property in a person's immediate possession is likely to be harmed or taken or

(2) to incite or provoke violence where there is a likelihood that such violence will ensue.

D.C. Code §22-1322, Rioting, provides:

(A) A riot . . . is a public disturbance involving an assemblage of 5 or more persons which by tumultuous and violent conduct or the threat thereof creates grave danger of damage or injury to property or persons.

Paragraph (B) creates criminal penalties for "Whoever willfully incites or urges other persons to engage in a riot."

President Trump violated none of these laws with his January 6 speech. That is readily apparent to anyone who listens to or reads the speech itself and who reads the law. But, don't take my word for it. One of the former Washington, D.C., prosecutors who enforced these laws so often he was dubbed the "protester prosecutor," a lawyer named Jeffrey Scott Shapiro, wrote an article for the *Wall Street Journal*, published on January 10, 2021, entitled, "*No, Trump Isn't Guilty of Incitement. Inflaming emotions isn't a crime. The president didn't mention violence, much less provoke it,*" wsj.com. In the article, Mr. Shapiro outlines what the law is and why President Trump did not come remotely close to violating it:

No, Trump Isn't Guilty of Incitement
Inflaming emotions isn't a crime. The president didn't mention violence, much less provoke it.

To the extent the Fake News Media and Democrats focused on President Trump's claims about the election irregularities and election fraud two observations are relevant: (1) this speech is political speech and "political speech is central to the meaning and purpose of the First Amendment," according to the United States Supreme Court. See *Virginia v. Black*, 538 U.S. 343 (2003) and (2) while many of President Trump's claims about the election irregularities are true (as I will demonstrate in an upcoming book), even if that were not the case, political speech is protected even if the speech is not true. See *U.S. v. Alvarez*, 567 U.S. 709 (2012).

Finally, 18 U.S.C. §2283 deals with "Rebellion or Insurrection." Previous versions of this statute are what Confederates and Southern participants in the Civil War were prosecuted under. Contending President Trump did anything to assist or engaged in a "Rebellion or Insurrection" in his January 6 speech is utterly ludicrous. In fact, as Jeffrey Scott Shapiro (the prosecutor who wrote the article above confirming President Trump did not violate any laws during his January 6 speech), notes in another opinion piece published in the *Wall Street Journal* on January 5, 2022, entitled, "*Stop Calling Jan. 6 an 'Insurrection,'*" the actions of the people who breached the U.S. Capitol buildings on January 6, 2021, do not constitute actual "insurrection" in the first place, as they were "unarmed and had no intention of overthrowing the U.S. constitutional system" and " a real insurrection would have required the armed forces to quell an armed resistance." See *wsj.com*:

Stop Calling Jan. 6 an 'Insurrection'

That's a legal term that denotes much more than a sporadically violent riot or disturbance.

Commentary: President Trump and millions of other Americans were understandably upset about the shenanigans that went on in the 2020 Presidential Election (which resulted in Joe Biden being certified as the winner of the election). Americans should be upset about it. As I will demonstrate in an upcoming book, the Democrats, with the help of the Fake News Media, a handful of leftist billionaires and some establishment Republicans, turned the 2020 United States Presidential Election into a farce. President Trump gathered with, and spoke to, thousands of other Americans on January 6, 2021 and urged them to PEACEFULLY SUPPORT the efforts of various Republican House and Senate members, and (the President hoped) Vice President Mike Pence, to challenge certification of the election. Nothing he said in any conceivable way incited any rioting or any effort to overthrow the United States Government (that is what rebellion and insurrection mean).

In truth, Democrat politicians routinely promote political violence, fighting and unrest. Here are a few illustrations. In 2017, Democrat U.S. Representative Maxine Waters proclaimed she would "take Trump out tonight." See *Breitbart*, "*Maxine Waters: 'I will go and take Trump out tonight,*" October 22, 2017, *breitbart.com*. (She claimed later she only wanted to impeach President Trump. See *AP News*, "*Maxine Waters: 'Take Trump Out' remark was about impeachment,*" October 24, 2017, *apnews.com*.)

A Democrat State Senator from Missouri publicly stated in 2017 that she hopes Trump is "assassinated." See *The Washington Post*, *"'I hope Trump is assassinated:' A Missouri lawmaker faces mounting calls to resign after Facebook comment,"* August 18, 2017, *washingtonpost.com*.

At a fundraiser in Philadelphia in 2008, then U.S. Senator Barack Obama, in reference to the GOP, claimed "If they bring a knife to the fight, we bring a gun." See *The Hill*, *"Obama on GOP: 'If They Bring a Knife to the Fight, We Bring a Gun,"* June 14, 2008, *thehill.com*.

In 2017, Democrat U.S. Senator Tim Kaine claimed Democrats needed to ". . . fight in Congress, fight in the courts and fight in the streets, fight online, fight at the ballot box" in opposition to the Trump Administration. See *CNS News*, *"Sen. Tim Kaine: 'We've Got to Fight in the Streets,"* October 16, 2018, *cnsnews.com*.

In 2018, Democrat U.S. Senator Cory Booker told supporters to "get in the face of some congresspeople." See *Fox News*, *"Sen. Cory Booker Pleads for Supporters to 'Get Up in the Face of Congresspeople,"* July 28, 2018, *foxnews.com*.

Sen. Booker followed that up in 2019, by claiming he sometimes feels like punching President Trump. See *The Hill*, *"Cory Booker: 'My testosterone sometimes makes me want to' punch Trump,"* July 23, 2019, *thehill.com*.

Additionally, who can forget the radical leftists who occupied the United States Senate Hart office building during the SCOTUS confirmation hearings for Judge Brett Kavanaugh? (Interesting, how that effort, fully supported by some Senate Democrats, was not hailed as an "insurrection," eh?) See *CBS News*, *"Anti-Kavanaugh protesters take over Senate building, Amy Schumer among those detained,"* October 4, 2018, *cbsnews.com*.

In short, as is oftentimes the case, President Trump was *falsely* accused of doing what the Democrats *actually* do. Now you know.

9

TRUMP WAITED 187 MINUTES TO CALL FOR PEACE ON JAN. 6?

No, he called for peace and calm within 25 minutes.

Additional Background: This Chapter deals with what is commonly referred to as "The January 6 Committee" or "J6 Committee." These monikers are short for the "*Select Committee to Investigate the January 6th Attack on the United States Capitol*" established by the Democrat majority in the United States House of Representatives. See *january6th.house.gov.* The Republican Party members in the United States House are not formally participating in the J6 Committee, after the Democrat Speaker of the House, Nancy Pelosi, refused to allow the House GOP Leader, Kevin McCarthy, to select all of the Republican representatives to serve on the panel. See *CBS News, "McCarthy pulls all Republicans from January 6 Select Committee after Pelosi rejects two picks,"* July 21, 2021, *cbsnews.com.* The J6 Committee consists of all Democrats and two Never Trump Republicans (who are participating without the approval of the Republican House Leader), Liz Cheney from Wyoming and Adam Kinzinger from Illinois. The willingness of Reps. Cheney and Kinzinger to serve on the J6 Committee, and their willingness to support what many observers view as an illegitimate committee, running roughshod over the rights of Americans, and their willingness to attack fellow Republicans, earned them a rare censure resolution from the Republican National Committee. See *Buzz Feed News*, *"The Republican National Committee Censured Liz Cheney And Adam Kinzinger,"* February 3, 2022, *buzzfeednews.com.*

The J6 Committee is supposed to be conducting an investigation into the January 6, 2021, U.S. Capitol riot. The J6 Committee came about after the effort to establish a formal commission was blocked in the United States Senate by Republicans. See *National Public Radio, "Senate Republicans Block A Plan for An Independent Commission On Jan. 6 Capitol Riot,"* May 28, 2021, *npr.org.*

The J6 Committee and its members engaged in some questionable conduct in their effort to build a narrative against President Trump surrounding the events of January 6, 2021. Here is an example.

THE FAKE NEWS

President Trump waited for 187 minutes to call for demonstrators to be peaceful after the Capitol was breached on January 6, 2021.

Who Pushed the Fake News?

The January 6 Committee itself on its Twitter™ feed and in interviews.

A tweet was posted to The January 6th Committee's official Twitter™ feed on January 3, 2022, claiming:

"It took Trump 187 minutes to make a statement calling off the mob that attacked our Capitol. The former President's dereliction of duty is cause for concern. @BennieGThompson"

Included in the post is a video of U.S. Representative Bennie Thompson, D–MS, being interviewed by Chuck Todd with NBC, where he repeats the same claim.

The claim has been promoted and repeated in other articles reporting on J6 Committee members. See *Yahoo Sports*, *"Rep. Liz Cheney says Trump sat in the White House dining room and watched the Capitol riot unfold on TV instead of taking immediate action to stop the violence,"* January 3, 2022, *sports.yahoo.com*.

THE TRUTH

Remember, President Trump called for peaceful protests *in the speech itself.* (See the previous Chapter.) Thereafter, President Trump appealed for peace from his supporters within 25 minutes of the breach of the Capitol Building or, if one starts the clock immediately after his speech ended, he called for peace within 88 minutes. See *The Federalist*, December 16, 2021, *thefederalist.com*:

J6 Committee Fabricates More Evidence, Says Trump Waited 187 Minutes To Call For Peace. It Was Actually 25

He did not wait over three hours to call for peace, as the J6 Committee falsely claims.

The January 6th Committee members, as politicians are inclined to do, do not state when they started the clock ticking to come up with the 187 minutes, but the timeline tells the story.

If one starts the clock ticking when the Capitol Building was "breached" (Though many people charged with illegally entering the Capitol Building on January 6 claim they were allowed into the building by law enforcement and the first January 6 defendant to be found not guilty of charges was acquitted on this basis. See *The Washington Post*, *"U.S. judge acquits Jan. 6 defendant who said he was waived in by police,*" April 6, 2022, *washingtonpost.com*), then President Trump waited 25 minutes to call for peace and calm. See *The Federalist* article cited above.

If one starts the clock ticking at the end of President Trump's January 6th speech at 1:10 p.m., he called for peace and calm in 88 minutes. See *The Federalist* article cited above.

Again, as noted above and in the previous Chapter, during his January 6, 2021 speech, President Trump called for his supporters to "peacefully and patriotically make their voices heard" when they walked to the Capitol Building to "cheer on our brave senators and congressmen and women." Therefore, he already called for peace during the speech itself.

If you watch the video interview of the January 6th Committee chairman, Rep. Bennie Thompson, referenced above in the Committee's Twitter™ feed, you will note Rep. Thompson claims President Trump was sitting in the White House the entire time. This is the same lie peddled by Rep. Liz Cheney in the *Yahoo Sports* article, *Yahoo Sports*, "*Rep. Liz Cheney says Trump sat in the White House dining room and watched the Capitol riot unfold on TV instead of taking immediate action to stop the violence,*" January 3, 2022, *sports.yahoo.com.*

Protesters entered the U.S. Capitol Building at 2:13 p.m., according to the timeline from *The New York Times* (see, "*How a Presidential Rally Turned Into a Capitol Rampage,*" January 12, 2021, *nytimes.com*), while *The Washington Post* records the time of the breach as 2:15 p.m. (See, "*How one of America's ugliest days unraveled inside and outside the Capitol,*" January 9, 2021, *washington-post.com.*) (One cannot rely on the NYT or WAPO for accuracy most of the time. These particular pieces of information, however, appear to be either correct or very close.)

At 2:38 p.m., President Trump tweeted:

Please support our Capitol Police and Law Enforcement. They are truly on the side of our Country. Stay peaceful!

See *The Federalist*, "*J6 Committee Fabricates More Evidence, Says Trump Waited 187 Minutes To Call For Peace. It Was Actually 25,*" December 16, 2021, *thefederalist.com*. The reader cannot pull up President Trump's Twitter™ post, since President Trump's account was suspended. The tweet is reproduced in *The Federalist* article.

About half an hour later, President Trump again addressed demonstrators on Twitter™ stating:

I am asking for everyone at the U.S. Capitol to remain peaceful. No violence! Remember, WE are the Party of Law & Order – respect the Law and our great men and women in Blue. Thank you!"

See *The Federalist* article cited above.

At 4:17 p.m., President Trump posted a video to his Twitter™ feed calling for protesters to "Go home" and stating "We have to have peace" and "Law and Order." See *The Federalist* article cited above, yet again. The video may be viewed at *C-Span*. See "*President Trump Video Statement on Capitol Protesters,*" January 6, 2021, *c-span.org*.

If one starts the clock running at the conclusion of President Trump's speech at 1:10 p.m., the 187 minute mark is reached at 4:17 p.m. Therefore, the January 6th Committee must be using the video posted by President Trump on his Twitter™ feed at 4:17 p.m. (though that tweet was suppressed by Twitter™), as the first call for peace. The Committee, however, ignores two previous tweets from President Trump calling for peaceful protests made hours earlier, as well as his call for peaceful protest made during the speech itself.

Commentary: Why would one Twitter™ post at 4:17 p.m., serve better to call for peace and calm than a Twitter™ post at 2:38 p.m. and another about 30 minutes later? Particularly, given the fact by 4:17 p.m., President Trump's Twitter™ account was already being suppressed by Twitter™? (See *The Federalist, "Twitter Locks Trump's Account, Threatens To Ban Him For Calling For Peace Following Capitol Riot,"* January 6, 2021, *thefederalist.com.*) Protesters would have been able to read President Trump's tweets calling for peace and calm made at 2:38 p.m. and 30 minutes later, but the J6 Committee goes on social media and on news programs ignoring those calls for peace and calm in order to create and perpetuate a gross misrepresentation of the President's actions. This is simply misinformation from the J6 Committee, but get ready because there is more of that to come.

10

GOP REP INSTRUCTED VP OVERTURN THE ELECTION?

No, not even close.

THE FAKE NEWS

A member of Congress texted President Trump's White House Chief of Staff Mark Meadows telling him to instruct Vice President Mike Pence to overturn the 2020 Presidential Election results.

Who Pushed the Fake News?

The January 6th Committee, formally known as the *Select Committee to Investigate the January 6th Attack on the United States Capitol* in a Committee hearing held on Monday, December 13, 2021.

At a January 6th Committee hearing held on the evening of Monday, December 13, 2021, J6 Committee member Adam Schiff (D–California) made a presentation by remote video feed. (See https://www.youtube.com/watch?v=Nxrg8dE 2Apo.)

During his presentation, Congressman Schiff put up a screenshot of what he claimed was a text from a lawmaker to Mark Meadows. At the time the text was supposedly sent, Mark Meadows was President Trump's White House Chief of Staff. The text was purportedly sent on January 5, 2021, the day before the Joint Session of Congress was to be presided over by Vice President Mike Pence when the Electoral College votes would be certified, thereby formally recognizing the next president.

Congressman Schiff presented a screenshot of the text claiming the text read as follows:

On January 6, 2021, Vice President Mike Pence, as President of the Senate, should call out all electoral votes that he believes are unconstitutional as no electoral votes at all.

See *YouTube*, at minute mark 1:05.

Congressman Schiff then goes on to state how critical it is that the Committee get to ask Mark Meadows about the text. Schiff then claims the lawmaker suggested the former Vice President simply "throw out votes he unilaterally deems unconstitutional in order to overturn a presidential election and subvert the will of the American people." See *YouTube* at 1:30.

THE TRUTH

What Mr. Schiff actually posted was a cropped, altered, partial text, omitting critical punctuation, omitting several additional texts all of which were sent together in a string, all the while adding in punctuation that was not in the text in his effort to mis-characterize the nature of the text.

In truth the text Schiff referred to was actually part of a string of three texts sent to U.S. Representative Jim Jordan (R-Ohio) by an attorney and former Department of Defense Inspector General, Joseph Schmitz. In the texts Mr.

FAKE NEWS EXPOSED ABOUT TRUMP

Schmitz provided a brief summary of a legal memorandum which was sent as an attachment to the texts. Rep. Jordan forwarded the string of texts to White House Chief of Staff Mark Meadows. See *The Federalist*, December 15, 2021, *thefederalist.com*:

During January 6 Hearing, Schiff Doctored Text Messages Between Mark Meadows And Rep. Jim Jordan

After *The Federalist* ran the original article calling out the improper revisions and Rep. Schiff's misstatements, a spokesperson for the January 6th Committee emailed *The Federalist* and admitted to manipulating the text. See *The Federalist*, December 15, 2021, *thefederalist.com*:

BREAKING: January 6 Committee Admits It Doctored Text Message Between Meadows And Jordan

The original texts sent to Rep. Jim Jordan by Mr. Schmitz, in fact, stated as follows:

"On January 6, 2021, Vice President Mike Pence, as President of the Senate, should call out all the electoral votes that he believes are unconstitutional as no electoral votes at all – in accordance with guidance from founding father Alexander Hamilton and judicial precedence"

"'No legislative act,' wrote Alexander Hamilton in Federalist No. 78, 'contrary to

the Constitution can be valid.' The court in Hubbard v. Lowe reinforced this truth: 'That an unconstitutional statute is not a law at all is a proposition no longer open to discussion.' 226 F. 135, 137 (SDNY 1915), appeal dismissed, 242 U.S. 654 (1916)."

"Following this rationale, an unconstitutionally appointed elector, like an unconstitutionally enacted statute, is no elector at all."

See *The Federalist,* "*During January 6 Hearing, Schiff Doctored Text Messages Between Mark Meadows and Rep. Jim Jordan,*" December 15, 2021, *thefederalist.com.* The legal memorandum attached to the texts sent to U.S. Rep. Jim Jordan and forwarded by Rep. Jordan to White House Chief of Staff Mark Meadows may be found at *everylegalvote.com.*

What U.S. Rep. Adam Schiff (or staff members acting on his behalf) did was alter the original text by cropping the last clause of the first text completely by deleting the phrase, "*in accordance with guidance from founding father Alexander Hamilton and judicial precedence*" and by deleting the "dash" after "votes at all" and replacing the dash with a period to create the misconception the sentence ended.

The text, as altered by Rep. Schiff is reproduced here:

LAWMAKER TEXT TO MEADOWS

On January 6, 2021, Vice President Mike Pence, as President of the Senate, should call out all electoral votes that he believes are unconstitutional as no electoral votes at all.

An image of the text, as doctored up by Rep. Schiff and the J6 Committee may also be found in *The Federalist* article cited above, as well as in the YouTube video of the J6 Committee hearing cited above.

While for a sitting member of the United States House of Representatives, who is also on the Committee supposedly "investigating" the events of January 6, 2021 in the Capitol, to alter a text in a manner which materially alters its meaning, is bad enough, Rep. Schiff then lied about the substance of the text itself and who it came from.

Schiff acted as though the text was an *instruction* or *command* from U.S. Rep. Jim Jordan commanding the White House Chief of Staff to instruct Vice President Pence on what to do on January 6, when in fact, the texts were forwarded by Rep. Jordan to Chief of Staff Meadows from an attorney informing anyone reading the text of legal precedent and authorities supporting the Vice President having the power to count the slates of electors he deemed to be legal. A more grotesque mis-characterization of the truth could scarcely be made.

Making matters worse still is the fact Rep. Adam Schiff used to be a Federal prosecutor. If Rep. Schiff will materially alter a colleague's text message and present the revised text as fact, then misrepresent what the text means, one cannot help but wonder what he would do with evidence in other contexts. That is a scary thought.

The Federalist articles referenced in this Chapter are interesting reads and do not paint very flattering pictures of U.S. Rep. Adam Schiff. Read them and you will have a good idea of just the sort of duplicitous, dishonest characters President Trump battled his entire term of office. And you will have a good idea of what to expect from the J6 Committee too.

Commentary: U.S. Rep. Adam Schiff has a long history of spreading misinformation and Fake News. During the height of the "Russia Collusion Hoax" he appeared on endless news shows and news broadcasts pushing the Democrat Party's "Russia, Russia, Russia" talking points and other misinformation. He weaponized his position on the *United States House Permanent Select Committee on Intelligence* to spread misinformation about President Trump and to attack President Trump endlessly.

It was Schiff's Committee which leaked emails from Donald Trump, Jr., *while Don, Jr., was in the process of testifying to the Committee*, about the hacked emails obtained from the Clinton Campaign, Democrat National Committee and Democrat Congressional Campaign Committee which were ultimately published by wikileaks before the 2016 Presidential Election. These leaks from the House Intelligence Committee led to the complete, utter Fake News reports that claimed Donald Trump, Jr., was notified of the wikileaks email dump before it happened, when in fact, he was notified after the fact. (This Fake News story is covered in Volume Two of this book series.)

Rep. Schiff was also one of the Impeachment Managers who presented the illegitimate Democrat Party claims in the First Impeachment of President Trump in January 2020. This is the same Rep. Schiff who literally fabricated quotes from President Trump during Schiff's opening statement in the Senate

Impeachment Hearing, quoting President Trump as saying to Ukrainian President Zelensky that he (Trump) wanted Zelensky to "make up dirt on my political opponent," when President Trump said no such thing. (This is also covered in The Federalist article cited above, *"During January 6 Hearing, Schiff Doctored Text Messages Between Mark Meadows and Rep. Jim Jordan,"* December 15, 2021, *thefederalist.com.*) Schiff later said his quotes were, in part, "parody." (You won't likely remember much about the First Impeachment of President Trump. That is because it was complete, utter hogwash and actually hurt the Democrat Party. Thus, the Dem Party leaders and their Fake News Media acolytes act like it never happened.)

Nevertheless, Rep. Schiff and company doctored up this most recent text message not only to allow them and the Fake News Media to spread misinformation, but also to obscure the fact that some legal scholars and attorneys, like Joseph E. Schmitz, the attorney who sent the memorandum to Rep. Jim Jordan (who then forwarded it to WH Chief of Staff Meadows) believed Vice President Pence did have the legal authority to choose the slates of electors or to request the States recertify.

Many people forget there were two sets of electors in seven swing states (known as "dueling electors") following the 2020 election. (See *Epoch Times*, *"Electors in 7 States Cast Dueling Votes for Trump,"* December 15, 2020, *theepochtimes.com.*) A good article about the "dueling electors" in the 2020 Presidential Elections was published by the *Association of Mature American Citizens.* See *"Explainer: Dueling Electors and the Upcoming Joint Session of Congress,"* December 17, 2020, *amac.us.* While prevailing with the GOP slate of "dueling electors" may have been an uphill battle, the effort did have some legal support.

Schiff and company want to obfuscate that fact (along with many other facts) and keep your attention diverted by spreading misinformation. The next time you hear or see anything from Rep. Adam Schiff or the J6 Committee, keep that in mind.

11

TEN PEOPLE DIED IN THE JAN. 6 RIOT?

Not exactly.

THE FAKE NEWS

Five or Seven or almost Ten people died in the January 6, 2021, Capitol riot.

Who Spread the Fake News?

A number of news media outlets and politicians ginned up and promoted (and continue to promote) this messaging. U.S. Representative Alexandria Ocasio-Cortez posted about this issue on October 24, 2021, on her Twitter™ feed:

Alexandria Ocasio-Cortez ✓
@AOC

Any member of Congress who helped plot a terrorist attack on our nation's capitol must be expelled.

This was a terror attack. 138 injured, almost 10 dead. Those responsible remain a danger to our democracy, our country, and human life in the vicinity of our Capitol and beyond.

The Democrat chairman of the dubious *Select Committee to Investigate the January 6th Attack on the United States Capitol*, U.S. Rep. Bennie Thompson (D-MS)(the guy with a long history of sympathizing with radical, violent black revolutionaries, yes, that guy), in a hearing in the United States House of Representatives in July 2021, claimed "We know seven people lost their lives" in the January 6, 2021, Capitol riot. See *The Washington Examiner*, "*The Jan. 6 commission hearings began with a falsehood*," July 27, 2021, *washingtonexaminer.com*.

In an article published on January 8, 2021, *The Guardian* framed the issue this way:

Capitol attack: the five people who died

Business Insider ran one of its versions of this story on January 23, 2021, as follows:

5 people died in the Capitol insurrection. Experts say it could have been so much worse.

CNN framed the issue this way in an article which ran on January 8, 2021:

What we know about the 5 deaths in the pro-Trump mob that stormed the Capitol

This gist of all of these political comments and articles is that January 6, 2021, was a dark, dangerous, deadly day striking at "the heart of American democracy," (in the words of the *CNN* article cited above). In order to make the events of January 6 seem deadlier and more dangerous than they actually were, the deaths of people in any way associated with the riot are related to it.

THE TRUTH

The fact is one person died January 6, 2021, either during, or as a direct result of the breach of the Capitol, and that person was a Trump supporter named Ashli Babbit, who was killed by Capitol police. One other person involved in the protest (but not the Capitol breach), Roseanne Boyland, may have died from the use of excessive force by police, though the D.C. Medical Examiner says she died of other causes. None of the people injured in the riot died from their injuries later.

See *The Washington Examiner* article entitled, "*Why do they keep inflating the Jan. 6 body count?*" October 26, 2021 *washingtonexaminer.com.*

Why do they keep inflating the Jan. 6 body count?

See also *The Washington Examiner,* "*The Jan. 6 commission hearings began with a falsehood,*" July 27, 2021, *washingtonexaminer.com.*

In addition, a Metropolitan Police Officer, Jeffrey Smith, was injured on January 6 while on duty and took his own life nine days later. In March 2022, his suicide was determined by the retirement board to be in the line-of-duty. See *WUSA*, "*DC officer who took his own life died in the line of duty, retirement board says*," March 9, 2022, *wusa9.com*.

To inflate the number of deaths on or pertaining to January 6, politicians and Fake News Media include people who died of strokes, heart attacks and drug overdoses that day and police officers who took their own lives days, weeks or even months later.

An examination of the individuals who passed away and who are included in the death tolls will inform the readers. These individuals are:

1. Ashli Babbitt. Ms. Babbitt was a 35 year old Air Force veteran who was shot and killed on January 6, 2021, by a Capitol police officer when she attempted to climb through the smashed out glass pane of a door leading to the "Speaker's Lobby" of the U.S. House of Representatives. See *Department of Justice Statement*, April 14, 2021, *justice.gov*.

In the words of Becket Adams, a reporter with *The Washington Examiner*, Ashli Babbitt is the only person whose death "was directly caused by the riot. No other deaths occurred during the attack. No one succumbed later to injuries sustained during the assault either." See *The Washington Examiner*, "*The Jan. 6 commission hearings began with a falsehood*," July 27, 2021, *washingtonexaminer.com*.

2. Capitol Police Officer Brian Sicknick. The untimely death of Officer Sicknick was the focus of a previous Chapter of this book. Readers will recall, the initial reports incorrectly blamed Officer Sicknick's death on injuries sustained in the Capitol Riot, however, autopsy results demonstrated he did not sustain any injuries and died of natural causes (strokes and a blood clot). See Chapter Seven.

3. Roseanne Boyland. *The New York Times* reported on January 15, 2021, that Ms. Boyland died due to being "trampled in a stampede" at the Capitol. See *"Videos Show How Rioter Was Trampled in Stampede at Capitol,"* January 15, 2021, *nytimes.com.* The *DC Medical Examiner* conducted an autopsy and determined Roseanne Boyland died of "acute amphetamine intoxication." See *The Washington Post, "D.C. medical examiner releases cause of death for four people who died during Capitol riot,"* April 7, 2021, *washingtonpost.com.* Roseanne Boyland may have actually been the victim of the use of excessive force and the use of noxious gas by Capitol police. See *American Greatness, "What Did the Capitol Celebrity Cops Do to Roseanne Boyland,"* September 6, 2021, *amgreatness.com.* (The Fake News Media doesn't want you to hear anything about that do they?)

4. Kevin Greeson. Mr. Greeson died of a heart attack on the Capitol grounds on January 6, 2021. See *WHNT, "Lawyer shares moments leading to heart attack that killed Athens man before Capitol siege,"* January 15, 2021, *whnt.com.* Mr. Greeson was also one of the four individuals mentioned in the misleading headline cited above in *The Washington Post.* The WAPO article confirms the medical examiner found Mr. Greeson died of "natural causes due to cardiovascular disease." See *The Washington Post, "D.C. medical examiner releases cause of death for four people who died during Capitol riot,"* April 7, 2021, *washingtonpost.com.*

5. Benjamin Phillips. Mr. Phillips was a 50 year old computer programmer, who also died of natural causes, specifically, hypertensive atherosclerotic cardiovascular disease, according to the DC Medical Examiner. He is another of the four people referenced in the misleading WAPO headline. See *The Washington Post, "D.C. medical examiner releases cause of death for four people who died during Capitol riot,"* April 7, 2021, *washingtonpost.com.* According to one of the individuals who rode with him to the Capitol that day, several people called Phillips when it was time to leave, but he did not appear. One of the calls to him was answered by police who informed the group Phillips had a stroke and died at George Washington University Hospital. See *Meaww,*

"Who was Benjamin Phillips? Pennsylvania man, 50, who died of stroke at Capitol riots created pro-Trump websites," January 8, 2021, *meaww.com.*

6. Capitol Police Officer Howard Liebengood, who was on duty at the Capitol on Jan. 6, took his own life on January 9, 2021. See *The Washington Post,* *"Capitol Police officer who was on duty during the riot has died by suicide, his family says,"* January 11, 2020, *washingtonpost.com.*

7. Metropolitan Police Officer Jeffrey Smith, who was also on duty at the Capitol on January 6, 2021, and who suffered injuries in the riot, took his own life on January 15, 2021. See *Yahoo News,* *"Another police officer committed suicide after US Capitol riot, Metropolitan police chief says,"* January 27, 2021, *news.yahoo.com.*

*Two additional Capitol Police Officers who were on duty on January 6, 2021, namely Officer Kyle DeFreytag and Officer Gunther Hashida, took their own lives on July 10, 2021 and July 29, 2021, respectively.

The simple fact is Trump Supporter Ashli Babbitt, who was killed by a Capitol Police Officer, is the only person who died in the breach of the Capitol on January 6, 2021. Further still, no other person involved in the actual Capitol breach died from the injuries they sustained on January 6, 2021. (Rosanne Boyland died outside of the Capitol in the west terrace tunnel.) Metropolitan Police Officer Jeffrey Smith was injured on January 6 and took his own life nine days later. The retirement board ruled his death was in the line of duty.

Commentary: In an effort to make the events of January 6, 2021, appear as deadly, dangerous and dramatic an "insurrection" as possible politicians and Fake News Media literally make up who was killed in it. Only Ashli Babbitt died after breaching the Capitol and she was shot by Capitol Police. One Metropolitan Police Officer, Jeffrey Smith, was injured on duty on January 6 and took his own life on January 15, 2021 for reasons determined to be in the line of duty.

The rest of the deaths touted by the January 6, doomsday pushers are further removed. Two Trump supporters, Kevin Greeson and Benjamin Phillips, died of natural causes (either heart attacks or strokes), one Capitol Police Officer, Brian Sicknick, died later of natural causes and one Trump supporter, Roseanne Boyland, died of in the west terrace tunnel, though as of this writing it is not entirely clear how. (Capitol police bodycam video shows an officer striking Boyland, who appears to be unconscious, with a stick or club. See *Epoch Times, "New Jan. 6 videos show DC police officer assaulting unconscious protester,"* April 29, 2022, *theepochtimes.com.*)

This must be the only "insurrection" in history, where people who died of natural causes during or after the "insurrection" itself are counted as casualties of it.

Further, after turning a blind eye to police officer suicides, suddenly the far-left politicians and Fake News Media claim every suicide of a law enforcement officer in the District of Columbia area is apparently the result of the January 6 riots. Many of these same far-left Democrats spent much of 2020, and thereafter, demonizing the police and calling to defund the police. (The Republican Study Committee has a clever video containing a collection of quotes, comments and videos from Democrats calling to defund the police. See *https://rsc-banks.house.gov/democrats-push-defund-police.* The Republican National Committee has seven minutes worth of videos of Democrat politicians, from U.S. Representatives to U.S. Senators to Governors, calling for defunding police. See *https://gop.com/video/7-minutes-of-democra ts-saying-defund-the-police/.*)

The sad fact is law enforcement officers have long suffered high rates of suicide. See *Police Executive Research Forum, An Occupational Risk: What Every Police Agency Should Do To Prevent Suicide Among Its Officers,* October 2019. See also, *Blue Help (bluehelp.org).* Until the events of January 6th, fringe leftist Democrats and the Fake News Media could not find a way to twist this fact to their benefit. So, for now, they will hype, embellish and dramatize this issue until they derive no further benefit from the topic, at least until the next Federal election is over or a high-profile police shooting puts them back on their usual message. Just watch.

12

7 HOURS OF WHITE HOUSE CALL LOGS ARE MISSING?

No, the White House switchboard call logs are complete.

THE FAKE NEWS

Official White House switchboard call logs from January 6, 2021 show a gap of over 7 hours in President Trump's communications from 11:17 a.m. to 6:54 p.m.

Who Pushed the Fake News?

The Washington Post "broke" the (non) story with an article published on March 29, 2022:

Jan. 6 White House logs given to House show 7-hour gap in Trump calls

The gist of the story is that the January 6 Committee (officially known, again, as the *Select Committee to Investigate the January 6th Attack on the United States Capitol*) obtained 11 pages of documents from the National Archives consisting of the president's "official daily diary" and the "White House switchboard call logs." According to the WAPO, the documents turned over to the January 6 Committee ". . . show a gap of seven hours and 37 minutes including the period when the building was being violently assaulted." See *washingtonpost.com*.

The article claims an unidentified lawmaker on the January 6 Committee said the Committee is investigating a "possible coverup of the official White House record from that day." See *washingtonpost.com*. Another "person close to the committee" said the "large gap" in the records is of "intense interest" to some lawmakers on the Committee.

CBS News posted its story the same day, March 29, 2022:

White House records turned over to House show 7-hour gap in Trump phone log on Jan. 6

Vanity Fair took the hyperbole to another level with its article also on March 29, 2022:

TRUMP'S MISSING PHONE LOGS MEAN WE DON'T EVEN KNOW HALF THE ILLEGAL SHIT HE MIGHT HAVE DONE ON 1/6

The Guardian ran its own version of the story on April 2, 2022:

What is Trump hiding? The Capitol riot-sized hole in White House call log

There are many more similar articles published by other media outlets such as *Business Insider*, "*White House call logs on the day of the Capitol riot had a 7-hour gap, report says, as House panel investigates 'possible cover-up'*," March 29, 2022, *businessinsider.com*, and *Newsweek*, "*What Trump Was Doing on Jan. 6 During Nearly 8-hour Gap in Phone Records*," March 29, 2022, *newsweek.com*, and more.

The gist of all of the articles is more or less the same. They claim there are missing White House phone logs covering over 7 hours of time on January 6, 2021 when the Capitol protests were on-going, that proof President Trump was on the phone extensively during this time period existed and there may be a "cover up" involving the President's communications that day.

The fact that Bob Woodward of Watergate fame was one of the reporters who "broke" this non-story in *The Washington Post* led to rampant claims from the left that the story of the supposedly "missing" 7 hours of phone logs from the White House on January 6, 2021, was "bigger" than Watergate and Nixon's 18 minutes of missing recordings.

THE TRUTH

The White House call logs and President's Daily Diary are complete for January 6, 2021. There is no "7 hour gap." The White House call logs only log calls made through the White House switchboard. Calls made from cell phones or landlines don't go through the switchboard and would not be contained in the switchboard call logs.

Additionally, the president's daily diary is not maintained by the President of the United States or anyone employed by him. The president's daily diary is compiled by an employee of the National Archives. Thus, these records upon which this non-story is partially based are not even generated by any president or his staff.

This is hard to fathom, but the media outlet which broke the true story was *CNN* in an article last updated on April 1, 2022, entitled, *"Official review of Trump phone logs from January 6 finds record is complete:"*

Official review of Trump phone logs from January 6 finds record is complete

As *CNN* reports in the article, "There are no missing pages and the seven-hour gap is likely explained by use of White House landlines, White House cell phones and personal cell phones that do not go through the switchboard."

See also, *The Washington Examiner*, April 1, 2022:

No missing pages from Jan. 6 White House switchboard logs: Report

And *The Federalist*, April 1, 2022:

April Fools! Gap In Trump's Jan. 6 Phone Records Was A Big Media-Fabricated Nothingburger

The truth was covered by other news media, including, but not limited to, *The Hill*, *"Official review found Jan. 6 White House phone records complete: report,"* March 31, 2022, *thehill.com*, and *American Thinker*, *"Oops! Another 'walls closing in' narrative about Trump hiding phone records with 7-hour 'gap' falls apart,"* April 1, 2022, *americanthinker.com.*

The problem is probably the antiquated White House telephone system. As *CNN* noted in its article debunking the original Fake News story, "The White House call log is generated by a switchboard system that dates back to the 1960s according to the National Archives."

As it turns out, calls from cell phones or direct calls from the Oval Office do not go through the White House Switchboard, as *CNN* confirms in the article.

You may recall the controversy in 2017 when the Trump Administration allegedly shut down the White House Comment Line and supposedly directed people to comment on Facebook. See *Addicting Info* (through Archive.Today), January 23, 2017. In truth, the Obama Administration shut down the White House Comment Line just weeks before President Trump's inauguration. See *The Washington Times*, "*White House shuts down call-in line*," January 14, 2017, *washingtontimes.com.* But, the Fake News that the Trump Administration shut down the comments line spread and resulted in some claims that the White House Switchboard was shut down. See *The Washingtonian*, "*White House Switchboard closed,*" January 23, 2017, *Washingtonian.com* (now with corrected headline reading, "*UPDATE: The White House Switchboard Isn't Closed, but its Comments Line is.*")

Why is that significant? Well, when *The Washingtonian* corrected its article about the White House Switchboard not being closed it noted, "A White House employee told *Washingtonian* the comments line has been closed since December but the switchboard is still open to take callers using *rotary-dial phones.*" (Emphasis added.) That system sounds rather antiquated doesn't it?

Along those lines, *electrospaces.net* published a good blog post on January 26, 2021, describing the different phones used in the Oval Office by President

Trump and President Biden. The post is titled, *"The phones in president Biden's Oval Office,"* and explains a good deal about White House communications. Note, the article states the modified Cisco 8851 IP phone on the president's desk (depicted in a photo in the article) went into service in 2016, is used for unclassified calls and connects to the White House switchboard where operators can direct the president's call to virtually anyone. (The web post contains a link to the *White House Switchboard* which takes one to *The White House Historical Association* page about White House Switchboard operators.)

The point is the White House switchboard system is apparently very old. Only some of the calls to and from the White House go through that system. Calls from White House land lines, White House cell phones and personal cell phones do not go through the switchboard and, therefore, will not wind up in the switchboard's call logs. That should surprise no one at all. There is no "gap" at all in the logs on January 6, 2021, just an absence of records from the White House switchboard where an absence of records is what one would expect, since many of the president's calls did not go through the switchboard.

Furthermore, the president's daily diary is not maintained by the president (not by any president). According to *The White House Historical Association*, the president's daily diary is compiled by the President's Diarist who is an employee of the <u>National Archives, NOT the White House</u>. (*CNN* references this in its report debunking the Fake News story.) According to *The White House Historical Association*, the president's daily diary is compiled from "information found in Secret Service logs, the president's schedule, notes from presidential staff members who track where he is."

<u>Commentary</u>: These Fake News stories were based on the White House <u>switchboard call logs</u> and the <u>president's daily diary</u>, according to the original article in *The Washington Post*. Obviously, the White House switchboard would not have received many of the calls coming in and out on any given day if the call did not come in to or go out through the switchboard. Additionally, President Trump and his staff did not even maintain the president's daily

diary, that is done by an employee of the National Archives.

What do you think the odds are the Fake News Media outlets spreading this misinformation knew many of the calls to and from the White House do not go through the antiquated switchboard system and that the president's daily diary is NOT maintained by the White House staff? The odds are pretty good aren't they? How legitimate is it to claim a "cover up" by President Trump based on logs of the outdated switchboard system and a daily diary that White House employees do not compile and President Trump does not control? This story was Fake News before it was put to print. Now you know the truth.

13

JAN. 6 RIOTERS TOOK ZIP TIES INTO CAPITOL TO TAKE LAWMAKERS HOSTAGE?

Not even close.

THE FAKE NEWS

On January 6, 2021, a couple of protesters at the Capitol brought zip ties into the Capitol building intending to take lawmakers hostage.

Who Pushed the Fake News?

This Fake News started circulating shortly after January 6. One of the earliest pieces on it was published by *Slate* on January 8, 2022:

They Were Out for Blood

The men who carried zip ties as they stormed the Capitol weren't clowning around.

The article claims the "zip tie guys" brought flex cuffs (another name for zip ties) into the Capitol and walked through the building "with a sense of purpose," with "military-ish precision" to the offices of Nancy Pelosi and to the Senate Floor. The article then references the supposed plan by right wing militia in Michigan to "kidnap" Michigan Governor Whitmer in 2020 and claims the men came "equipped to take hostages," and to "physically seize officials." See *slate.com.*

(We now know the Whitmer "kidnapping plot" was an FBI-inspired, planned and orchestrated scheme to entrap some Michigan militia members into a ridiculous plan to "kidnap" the Michigan Governor is 2020. A Federal criminal jury completely acquitted two of the defendants charged in this questionable "plot" and failed to convict the other two. The case was defended on entrapment grounds primarily. See *The Federalist*, "*Jury Refuses To Convict Men Entrapped By FBI In Whitmer Kidnapping Plot,*" April 8, 2022, *thefederalist.com* and *American Greatness*, "*Two Acquitted in Whitmer case, FBI Misconduct Central,*" April 8, 2022, *amgreatness.com.*)

One of the "zip tie guys" was Eric Munchel who traveled to Washington that day with his mother. See *The Washington Post*, "*Man photographed in Capitol with zip-tie cuffs and his mother win pretrial release in case that tested federal riot protections,*" March 29, 2021, *washingtonpost.com*. (Because violent revolutionaries always take their mom along for the mayhem, right?)

In the case of another "zip tie guy," retired Air Force Lt. Colonel Larry Rendall Brock, Jr., the story he went to the Capitol armed with zip ties to take hostages or even to attempt to "execute members of the U.S. Government" was actually made in Federal Court by a Federal Prosecutor on January 14, 2021. Naturally, the news media eagerly spread the story. See *AP News*, January 14, 2021:

Prosecutor: Capitol rioter aimed 'to take hostages'

THE TRUTH

Eric Munchel did not carry zip ties to the Capitol at all. He found the zip ties in the Capitol building itself as he wandered around. This fact was admitted by the Federal Prosecutors in a filing made on January 20, 2021, wherein the prosecutors claimed he "gleefully acquired several sets of plastic handcuffs as he walked through the Capitol —." (See pg. 1.) See also, *Yahoo News*, January 21, 2021, *yahoo.com* and *Insider*, "*The Capitol riot's 'zip tie guy' appeared to take the plastic handcuffs from Capitol police, prosecutors say*," January 21, 2021, *insider.com*:

The Capitol riot's 'zip-tie guy' appeared to take the plastic handcuffs from Capitol police, prosecutors say

The other "zip tie guy," retired Air Force Lt. Colonel Larry Rendall Brock, Jr., also claimed, in an interview with Ronan Farrow of the *New Yorker*, see "*An Air Force Combat Veteran Breached The Senate*," published on January 8, 2021, that he picked up the zip ties from the floor of the Capitol building after entering. See *newyorker.com*.

While the Federal prosecutor handling Brock's case claimed the retired Air Force Lieutenant Colonel intended to "take hostages" or even "execute" members of the U.S. Government, an FBI agent who testified at the pretrial detention hearing on January 14, 2021, admitted retired Air Force officer could have picked up the zip ties while in the Capitol, rather than bringing them

JAN. 6 RIOTERS TOOK ZIP TIES INTO CAPITOL TO TAKE LAWMAKERS...

in. See *Fox News*, *"Air Force vet seen in Capitol with zip ties intended 'to take hostages," prosecutor says,"* January 15, 2021, *foxnews.com.*

Of significance in this context is the United States Department of Justice's admission in other cases of the lack of evidence that January 6 protesters intended to "capture" and/or "assassinate" anyone. This "walk back" started as early as January 15, 2021. See *NBC News*, January 15, 2021:

Federal official walks back allegation rioters intended to 'capture and assassinate'

The best proof Eric Munchel and Larry Rendall Brock, Jr., did not enter the Capitol grounds to take hostages or kill any government personnel is they are not charged with any such crimes. While both are charged with a litany of disorderly conduct charges, obstructing official proceedings and entering and remaining in restricted buildings, neither is charged with violating 18 USC §1201, the Federal Kidnapping statute or with conspiracy to commit a violation of that statute or with violating 18 USC §1114, the Federal statute protecting the lives of Federal officials. See *U.S. Department of Justice, Eric Gavelek Munchel case update, justice.gov* and *U.S. Department of Justice, Larry Rendall Brock case update, justice.gov.* Considering the extent to which the Federal Government is "throwing the book" at every Jan. 6 defendant they charge, rest assured they would charge Munchel and Brock, Jr., with kidnapping and anything else they could conceive of if they had even the slightest justification.

Commentary: The fable that Eric Munchel and Larry Brock, Jr., came to the U.S. Capitol on January 6, 2021, with "zip ties" or "flex cuffs" with the intent to take Federal legislators "hostage" or even to "execute" them fit perfectly into both the Fake News Media, Democrats and Federal Government's effort to grossly mischaracterize, sensationalize and over hype the events which transpired at the Capitol that day. This over-dramatization and the grossly over-sensationalized claims about January 6, bolster the even more over-the-top claims of Democrat politicians about January 6, like Vice President Kamala Harris who equated the January 6, 2021, Capitol protests with the attack by the Japanese on Pearl Harbor on December 7, 1941 (*See USA Today,* "*Kamala Harris speech: January 6 will 'echo' in U.S. history like Pearl Harbor, 9/11,*" January 6, 2022, *usatoday.com*) or to the 9/11 terror attacks or President Joe Biden who claimed January 6 was "the worst attack on our democracy since the Civil War." (See *The New York Post,* "*Biden ripped for calling Capitol riots 'worst attack on our democracy since the Civil War,*" April 29, 2021, *nypost.com.*)

If the Federal Government had ANY proof whatsoever that either of these guys went to Washington on January 6, 2021, with the intent to kidnap, harm or assassinate any Federal official of any kind, you better believe these two would be charged with every conceivable related charge the U.S. Attorney's office could conjure. The fact neither man faces any such charges confirms the Government possesses absolutely no evidence whatsoever supporting any such charges. News media interested in fairly reporting on these two cases would immediately note the lack of charges corresponding to such serious offenses, don't you think?

The first casualty of The Fake News Media and leftist politicians is the truth. The relentless efforts by Fake News Media and prominent Democrat politicians to mischaracterize and over-dramatize the events of January 6 are stark reminders of this fact.

14

$30 MILLION IN DAMAGE WAS DONE BY JAN. 6 RIOT?

No, the actual property damage done by the rioters was a fraction of that.

THE FAKE NEWS

The January 6, 2021, protesters did $30 million dollars in damage to the Capitol.

Who Pushed the Fake News?

This particular piece of Fake News is derived from the *Architect of the Capitol*, J. Brett Blanton's, Statement before the U.S. House of Representatives Committee on Appropriations hearing on February 24, 2021.

National Public Radio ran its version of the story on February 24, 2021, *npr.org*:

Architect Of The Capitol Outlines $30 Million In Damages From Pro-Trump Riot

The New York Times also ran its version of the story on February 24, 2021, *nytimes.com*:

Capitol Riot Costs Will Exceed $30 Million, Official Tells Congress

CBS News ran its story on the same day, *cbsnews.com*:

More than $30 million needed for Capitol repairs and new security after assault, officials say

There are many more similar stories, but these are representative. The gist is the Capitol protests on January 6, 2021, were extremely destructive and did tens of millions of dollars in damage to the Capitol grounds and Capitol buildings.

The New York Times did note in its article cited above that the $30,000,000.00 figure included not only repairs costs for physical damage, but also the costs of increased security and "mental health services" for traumatized government employees. Most of the articles on this topic also mention the cost of funding the perimeter fencing around the Capitol and the potential for the costs to go higher if the fencing were needed beyond March 31, 2021.

THE TRUTH

The cost of the actual damage done to the U.S. Capitol during the protests and breach of the Capitol buildings on January 6, 2021, is somewhere between $1.5 million and $2.73 million, according to the Federal Government.

The original estimates of the costs of the damage to the Capitol of $1,495, 326.55 million were made public for the first time in a *plea agreement* (see pg. 8 of the plea agreement) and sentencing hearing for Paul Allard Hodgkins on Wednesday, June 2, 2021. See also, *The Washington Post, "Tampa man pleads guilty to felony in Jan. 6 Capitol riot; his recommended prison sentence could set bar for other cases,"* June 2, 2021, *washingtonpost.com* and *American Greatness, "Another January 6 Falsehood: $30 Million in Damages to the Capitol,"* June 7, 2021, *amgreatness.com:*

Another January 6 Falsehood: $30 Million in Damages to the Capitol

If the day was as bad as authorities say, why do they have to keep lying about what happened?

Later, in a *Sentencing Memorandum* filed by the U.S. Department of Justice on April 8, 2022, in the case involving defendant Anthony Vuksanaj, the costs "incurred as a result of the damage caused by the Capitol Siege," were estimated to be $2,734,783.14. (See pg. 15, footnote 3.) See also, *Forbes, "Capitol Riot Costs Go Up. Government Estimates $2.73 million in Property Damage,"* April 8, 2022, *forbes.com.*

As it turns out, the damage done to the U.S. Capitol was not nearly as extensive as the Fake News Media breathlessly reported. In fact, given the United States Government's ability literally burn through tens of millions, even tens of billions of dollars, in every pursuit it undertakes, one must question exactly what damage was actually done if $2.73 million in actual damages incurred is all the Feds can conjure.

Commentary: In June 2021, the Federal Government estimated the approximate costs of damage to the United States Capitol was $1,495,326.55. As of April 8, 2022, the Federal Government estimated the costs "incurred" as a result of the damage caused the Capitol protests was $2,734,783.14. Those numbers are a far cry from the $30,000,000.00 price tag bandied about by the media shortly after the Architect of the Capitol's presentation to Congress. The additional $27,200,000.00 is an incredible sum to spend on traumatized employees "mental health counseling" is it not?

Never underestimate the ability of the Federal Government to wantonly waste money, though. Remember, how the Biden Administration needlessly kept the National Guard deployed in Washington, D.C., for over two months after January 6, 2021? That cost around $500,000,000 dollars, according to the U.S. Department of Defense. See *WUSA9*, "*Price tag hits almost $500 million for the National Guard's response to the Insurrection,*" February 9, 2021, *wusa9.com.* (That one WUSA9 story epitomizes the hyperbolic Fake News and misinformation surrounding the January 6 riot. First, the episode was not an "insurrection" – that is covered in the next Chapter of this book – and, second, the National Guard did not remain in D.C. for over four months after the end of a riot that lasted a few hours on Jan. 6, because of the riot. Democrats and Republicans alike wanted the National Guard to leave long before it did. See *Business Insider*, "*Lawmakers from both sides criticize the Pentagon over its decision to station the National Guard at the Capitol until May,*" March 14, 2021, *businessinsider.com.*)

At least one Federal judge presiding over a January 6 defendant's case wondered why the restitution requested by the Feds was only $500.00 for misdemeanors and $2,000.00 for felonies when the supposed cost of the riot totaled over $500 million. See *The Hill*, "*Judge asks why restitution in Capitol riot cases is capped*," August 10, 2021, *thehill.com*.

Nevertheless, the point is simple: once again, when it comes to the January 6 protests and Capitol breach, the damage to the Capitol, like every other aspect of the events of that day, is grossly embellished and sensationalized.

15

JAN. 6 WAS AN "ARMED INSURRECTION" TO "OVERTHROW THE GOVERNMENT?"

Not even close.

THE FAKE NEWS

The January 6, 2021 Capitol protests and Capitol breach were an armed insurrection to overthrow the United States Government.

Who Pushed the Fake News?

This particular Fake News narrative is pushed extensively by numerous media outlets and politicians. Different parts of the narrative are pushed by Fake News Media at various times. Cumulatively, their combined hyperbolic stories craft the narrative the Capitol protests were an armed attempt at sedition, rebellion or a "coup" to overthrow the Government.

American Oversight claimed the January 6 protesters were a "heavily armed mob" who "stormed the U.S. Capitol" in an "attempted coup." See *americanoversight.org*:

THE JANUARY 6 ATTACK ON THE U.S. CAPITOL

The heavily armed, Trump-incited mob attack of Jan. 6, 2021, was an attack not just on the U.S. Capitol building, but also on democracy and the rule of law.

USA Today, see *usatoday.com,* published an opinion piece on January 4, 2022 entitled:

What if the Jan. 6 insurrection had succeeded in illegally installing Trump?

President Joe Biden called the January 6, 2021 riot, "an attempted coup" during a speech on January 11, 2022. See *The Hill,* "*Biden calls Jan. 6 riot an attempted 'coup',*" January 11, 2022, *thehill.com.*

The Nation out did itself and likened the Capitol Riot to Adolf Hitler and the German National Socialists Workers Party's beer hall putsch in an article published on January 3, 2022. See *thenation.com:*

The Uncanny Resemblance of the Beer Hall Putsch and the January 6 Insurrection

(The left is simply never content until they liken someone to Hitler or Nazi Germany.)

To make the Capitol Riot look like an armed uprising, the Fake News Media dramatize and mislead regarding the weapons carried by some of the rioters.

On January 16, 2021, *The Hill* ran an article with the following title (see *thehill.com*):

Police seized alarming number of weapons on Capitol rioters, court documents show

On January 13, 2021, *NBC News* ran a story with the following headline (see *nbcnews.com*):

Stun guns, 'stinger whips' and a crossbow: What police found on the Capitol protesters

In all, police recovered a dozen guns and thousands of rounds of ammunition from seven people who were arrested before and after the Capitol riot.

On January 14, 2021, *Esquire* framed the "armed insurrection" as follows (see *esquire.com*):

The Catalogue of Deadly Weaponry Among Capitol Insurrectionists Is Astonishing

On the first anniversary of the January 6 Capitol Riot, President Joe Biden called the event an "armed insurrection." See *AFP News Agency YouTube™* page, "*Biden calls Capitol riot an 'armed insurrection'*," January 6, 2022.

In an article published on January 30, 2021, *Vogue* proclaimed (see *vogue.com*):

Republicans Are Over the Armed Insurrection of the Capitol. But We Can't Be.

Even academic groups joined in on pushing the narrative. A good illustration is *The Berkshire Conference of Women Historians* which issued a statement on January 10, 2021, calling the January 6 protesters "seditionists who committed treason and attempted to overthrow the US government." See *berksconference.org*. (This group also claimed in the same statement that the United States is a nation founded on the ideals of "white supremacy" and the January 6 crowd was able to "occupy the Capitol because white supremacy allows white people to move freely, rebel and inhabit their —bodies and state spaces – in ways denied racialized people in the US." Wow. That is some radical leftist nonsense. The notion a group of professional academics publicly released such a twisted statement is hard to fathom, but there it is for all to read.)

There is literally an endless stream of similar stories, broadcasts, web articles and other media along these lines. The point is the Fake News Media is all-hands-on-deck to try to paint the events of January 6, 2021, in the most violent, radical, extreme manner possible while leading the public to believe the Capitol Riot was an organized effort by a mob of radical right wingers armed with guns to overthrow the Federal Government. That is what all of the rhetoric, hyperbole and sensationalism appears to be about.

THE TRUTH

If one considers an "armed insurrection" to "overthrow the Government" to be an event orchestrated by an organized group of people armed with guns who actually intend to overthrow the Government, then, no, the January 6, 2021, Capitol Riot was no such thing.

In short, the Capitol Riot was exactly that, a riot.

Armed Insurrection?

Not one single person has been arrested or charged with entering the Capital Building with a firearm on January 6, 2021.

Not one single person has been arrested or charged with discharging (shooting) a firearm in connection with the January 6, 2021, Capitol protests.

In fact, the only shot fired in connection with the Capitol protests was the shot fired by Capitol Police Lt. Michael Byrd who shot and killed protester Ashli Babbit.

Only a handful of people in any way associated with the Capitol protests were arrested for even illegally possessing firearms in the District of Columbia (which has very strict gun laws) on January 6, 2021, and there is zero evidence any of these individuals pulled a gun, shot a gun or used a gun that day.

Of the over 800 people charged with crimes as a result of the Capitol Riots (as of this writing) only a fraction (by this writer's count, less than 100) were armed with any weapons at all and the vast majority of those were flag poles (yes, people who came to the protests with flag poles are being charged with using the flag poles as weapons), pepper spray, bats, walking sticks, crutches and similar items.

See *American Greatness*, February 19, 2021, *amgreatness.com*:

No Proof January 6 Was an 'Armed Insurrection'

Byron York, chief political correspondent with *The Washington Examiner*, wrote an enlightening article on the subject in October 2021 (see *washingtonexaminer.com*):

'Armed insurrection': What weapons did the Capitol rioters carry?

After an exhaustive look through the Federal charges pending against people associated with the January 6, 2021, Capitol Riot, he wrote:

"By any current American standard of civil disorder, what happened Jan. 6 was a riot. There was fighting. There was property destruction. There were some instigators, and there were many more followers. And as the day went on, some people lost their heads and did things they should regret for a very long time.

But a look at the Justice Department prosecutions simply does not make the case that it was an "armed insurrection."

See *thewashingtonexaminer.com*.

Regarding the issue of "insurrection" former Federal prosecutor Jeffrey Scott Shapiro wrote an opinion piece in the *Wall Street Journal* on January 5, 2022, entitled "*Stop Calling Jan. 6 an 'Insurrection*," see *wsj.com*. In the article, the former Federal prosecutor for the District of Columbia explains why the riot on January 6 was not an "insurrection:"

OPINION | COMMENTARY
Stop Calling Jan. 6 an 'Insurrection'
That's a legal term that denotes much more than a sporadically violent riot or disturbance.

On March 4, 2021, Jill Sanborn, assistant director of the FBI counter-terrorism division, testified to a U.S. Senate Committee that the FBI did not recover any firearms "on that day from any of the arrests at the scene at this point," though she could not speak for Metro and Capitol police. See *USA Today*, *"Fact check: Claim about FBI official who said bureau recovered no guns at Capitol riot is missing context,"* March 4, 2021, *usatoday.com*. (Context? The FBI agent testified the Feds recovered no guns and the only shot fired was by the Capitol police officer who shot Ashli Babbit.)

As for the people charged with firearm-related charges arising out of the January 6 Capitol Riot? There are five such individuals, as of this writing:

1. Christopher Michael Alberts (He was arrested on Jan. 6, at 7:25 p.m., several hours after the riot was over, carrying a handgun on his person. See *justice.gov*, press release containing Complaint/Arrest Warrant. He is not charged with using the firearm in any way.)

2. Lonnie Leroy Coffman (On Jan. 6, he had a gun on his person and several in his vehicle, along with some jars filled with jellied gasoline. See *justice.gov*, press release containing Complaint/Arrest Warrant. He is not charged with brandishing the weapons or using them in any way.)

3. Mark Sam Ibrahim (At the time he was a DEA agent who was on leave and carried his Drug Enforcement Agency issued sidearm at the protests on January 6. See *CBS News*, *"Ex-DEA Agent From Orange County, Mark Sami Ibrahim, Charged In Connection With Jan. 6 Capitol Riot,"* July 20, 2021, *cbsnews.com*. He is not charged with using the firearm in any way.)

4. Cleveland Grover Meredith, Jr. (He was not even at the January 6 Capitol Riot. He arrived in DC the following day and was arrested on January 7 in the possession of firearms in DC. See *Statement of Offense* filed *in United States of America vs. Cleveland Grover Meredith*, docket no. 1:21-cr-00159.)

5. Guy Wesley Reffitt (He was charged with illegally carrying a firearm at the Jan. 6 Capitol Riot. He did not use the firearm. He was on the Capitol grounds, but did not enter the Capitol Building. He is the first Jan. 6 defendant tried and convicted. He was convicted on March 8, 2022 of various charges, but was not even charged with assaulting anyone or

using a firearm on anyone.)

The U.S. Attorney's press release states he was convicted of the following:

"The jury found Reffitt guilty of five charges, including two counts of civil disorder, and one count each of obstruction of an official proceeding, entering and remaining in a restricted building or grounds with a firearm, and obstruction of justice."

The U.S. Attorney's press release confirms Reffitt did not enter the Capitol buildings:

"As he kept moving, Reffitt urged others to keep moving forward, too. He eventually made it up the stairs to outside the Senate wing of the Capitol, as others breached the building, but he did not personally go inside."

See *United States Department of Justice Press Release, "Texas Man Found Guilty by Jury of Felony Charges for Actions Related to Capitol Breach,"* March 8, 2022, *justice.gov.*

Not one person remotely involved in the Capitol Riot is charged with shooting anyone or even pulling a gun on January 6.

Overthrow the Government?

If the Capitol Riot was an effort to overthrow the United States Government one would expect for at least a few people to be charged with conspiring to overthrow the government right? After all, a specific Federal statute, 18 U.S.C. §2384, deals precisely with such a crime, though as we will see, the statute is broader than that.

Of the over 800 people charged with Capitol Riot-related offenses, how many are charged with Seditious Conspiracy to Overthrow the United States

Government? The answer is ZERO (as of this writing in May 2022).

The only individuals charged with violating 18 U.S.C. §2384 are the Oath Keepers. See *American Greatness*, *"The Pathetic and Political Sedition Case Against the Oath Keepers,"* January 20, 2022, *amgreatness.com*. But, they are not charged with attempting to overthrow the government and they are not charged with firearms violations.

18 U.S.C. §2384, the "Seditious Conspiracy" statute, provides:

"If two or more persons in any State or Territory, or in any place subject to the jurisdiction of the United States, conspire to overthrow, put down, or to destroy by force the Government of the United States, or to levy war against them, or to oppose by force the authority thereof, or *by force to prevent, hinder, or delay the execution of any law of the United States*, or by force to seize, take, or possess any property of the United States contrary to the authority thereof, they shall each be fined under this title or imprisoned not more than twenty years, or both." (Emphasis Added.)

Readers will note, the statute criminalizes not only conspiring to "overthrow, put down or to destroy by force the Government of the United States," but also conspiring to "by force to prevent, hinder or delay the execution of any law of the United States . . .."

A review of the criminal indictment against the Oath Keepers reflects they are charged with violating 18 U.S.C. §2384, but NOT with trying to overthrow the government. According to the Oath Keepers' indictment the purpose of the conspiracy was ". . . *to oppose the lawful transfer of presidential power by force, by preventing, hindering, or delaying by force the execution of the laws governing the transfer of power.*" See Pg. 8, Paragraph 16.)(Emphasis Added.)

Thus, the only people charged with Seditious Conspiracy arising out of the events of January 6, 2021, are the Oath Keepers, but even they are not charged with trying to overthrow the Federal Government. Importantly, none of the Oath Keepers indicted in connection with the January 6 Capitol Riot are charged with firearms violations. They did not have any guns in the District of Columbia on January 6. See *American Greatness*, *"The Pathetic and Political Sedition Case Against the Oath Keepers,"* January 20, 2022, *amgreatness.com.* (The indictment also confirms there are no firearms violations among the charges and no firearms were used by Oath Keepers in DC that day, though the indictment claims the group moved weapons to a location in Virginia.)

Simply stated, the Capitol Rioters were not armed with guns and did not use any guns during the riot. Only a handful of people who even attended the rallies had guns and an even tinier number of those individuals had anything to do with the riot itself. What transpired on January 6, 2021 at our National Capitol did not remotely rise to the level of "armed insurrection." There is literally no proof whatsoever the Capitol rioters intended to, or were capable of, "overthrowing" the United States Government or perpetrating a coup. The Fake News Media's shrill cries to the contrary are simply ridiculous.

Commentary: A handful of people who attended the rallies at the Capitol on January 6 had guns either in their vehicles or on their person. An even smaller number of people apparently participated in the Capitol Riot while possessing a firearm. *No one is charged with entering the Capitol Building with a firearm. No one involved in the Capitol Riots is charged with shooting anyone or even pointing a gun at any one.* Yet, the Fake News Media endlessly squawk about the riot being an "armed insurrection." That is misleading simply because when the average person hears "armed insurrection" in a news report or reads "armed insurrection" in a headline, those words conjure images of people storming the Capitol with guns. That simply did not happen.

A small percentage of the people involved in the Capitol Riots carried non-lethal weapons, such as canes, walking sticks, flag poles, pepper spray and similar items. The Fake News Media uses this fact, coupled with the relentless over-hype and embellishment about the handful of people charged with possessory gun offenses, to mischaracterize the events of January 6, 2021, as a heavily armed mob intent on overthrowing our government.

In truth, many of the pro-Trump supporters who attended the January 6 rallies probably carried non-lethal weapons due to the likelihood of leftist Antifa attacks, as Antifa and other leftists routinely attack Trump supporters and conservatives. For a few illustrations of radical leftist violence aimed at Trump supporters, see:

The Washington Post, "*Ugly, bloody scenes in San Jose as protesters attack Trump supporters outside rally,*" June 3, 2016, *washingtonpost.com.*

ABC 3340 News, "*Trump says 'ANTIFA SCUM' attacked supporters at DC rallies,*" November 15, 2020, *abc3340.com.*

The Los Angeles Times, "*Southern California anti-fascists charged with violently countering pro-Trump 'Patriot March,*" December 7, 2021, *latimes.com.*

VOA News, "*Antifa Protester Implicated in Killing of Trump Supporter in Oregon,*" September 1, 2020, *voanews.com.*

The handful of people charged with possession firearms on January 6 claimed the firearms were for self-defense as well.

As for sedition, rebellion or overthrowing the government, not one single person among the more than 800 charged in connection with the January 6 Capitol Riots are charged with any such offense. The closest such charges are against the Oath Keepers and they are charged with conspiring to delay the execution of the law by force, not with overthrowing the government or with attempting a coup.

(If you are interested *Insider* maintains a "searchable table" of the individuals charged with January 6 related offenses. See *https://www.insider.com/al*

l-the-us-capitol-pro-trump-riot-arrests-charges-names-2021-1. The *U.S. Department of* Justice also has what it calls a *"U.S. Capitol Breach Investigation Resource Page"* with links to the individuals charged and other information. See *https://www.justice.gov/usao-dc/capitol-breach-investigation-resource-pa ge.*)

The January 6 Capitol protests ultimately turned into a riot. That by itself is bad enough without all of the balderdash, exaggerations and embellishment. The claims this ragtag assortment of people, a small portion of which carried flag poles and pepper spray, were intent on overthrowing the U.S. Government or ending our Republic are ludicrous.

Beginning with Donald Trump's run for office in 2015 and throughout his Presidency on through to the present day, the Fake News Media and Democrat politicians denied or downplayed the leftist violence aimed at Trump supporters and conservatives. Throughout the George Floyd and BLM protests of 2020 and 2021, the same Fake News Media and Democrat politicians denied or downplayed the leftist violence and riots perpetrated all over this Country, including those which targeted Federal Courthouses and other Federal Buildings. All of those violent assaults and riots were no cause for alarm to the Fake News Media. This one riot involving Trump supporters, however, is another matter. Though the property damage and violence of the Capitol Riot pales in comparison to some of the BLM riots (see *The New York Post,* "*Riots following George Floyd's death may cost insurance companies up to $2B,*" September 16, 2020, *nypost.com*), the Capitol Riot is hyped, embellished and mischaracterized. All of this is done for political reasons, not because of what actually happened in the riots at issue. The Fake News Media coverage of the Capitol Riot make that fact crystal clear.

16

TRUMP SAYS "HANG MIKE PENCE" IS "COMMON SENSE?"

No, he did not.

THE FAKE NEWS

In an interview with ABC chief Washington correspondent Jonathan Karl in November 2021, President Trump defended or justified the fact some Jan. 6 protesters were chanting "Hang Mike Pence," as "common sense."

Who Pushed the Fake News?

Axios led the charge with this article on November 12, 2021:

Exclusive audio: Trump defends threats to "hang" Pence

The article claims President Trump "quite extensively" defended supporters who threatened to "hang" former Vice President Mike Pence. The story includes a transcript of 36 seconds of a 90 minute interview.

Business Insider published its version on November 12, 2021, entitled:

Trump justified his supporters calling to hang Mike Pence at the Capitol riot, saying it's 'common sense' in new audio

Also on November 12, 2021, *NBC News* published its own version of the story:

Trump defends Jan. 6 rioters' 'hang Mike Pence' chant in new audio

The version promoted by *The Guardian* on November 12, 2021 read:

Trump defended rioters who threatened to 'hang Mike Pence', audio reveals

Virtually every Fake News outlet in America ran with this story, but those cited above are representative. The stories all basically claim President Trump justified and/or defended protesters shouting "hang Mike Pence" by saying it was "common sense." As is usually the case, the Fake News Media takes liberties with what President Trump actually said.

THE TRUTH

In the interview, Jonathan Karl interjected the "hang Mike Pence" observation after President Trump was already expressing thoughts after answering a previous question. Karl did NOT EVEN ASK President Trump a question about the "hang Mike Pence" chant.

FAKE NEWS EXPOSED ABOUT TRUMP

The Federalist published an article on November 12, 2021, breaking the issue down and exposing the Media lies for what they are:

Trump Never Defended Calls To 'Hang Mike Pence,' But Shameless Media Can't Stop Lying About It

Here is how the transcript would read if accurately reported:

Jonathan Karl:

Were you worried about him during that siege? Were you worried about his safety?

Donald Trump:

No, I thought he was well protected and I had heard he was in good shape.No. Because I had heard he was in very good shape. But, but, no, I think—

Jonathan Karl:

Because you heard those chants – that was terrible. I mean, you know ....

Donald Trump:

He could have – well the people were very angry.

Jonathan Karl:

They were saying hang

Donald Trump:

FAKE NEWS EXPOSED ABOUT TRUMP

Because it's –

Jonathan Karl:

. . . Mike Pence–

Donald Trump:

. . . common sense Jon. It's common sense that you are supposed to protect. How can you – if you know a vote is fraudulent right? How can you pass on a fraudulent vote to Congress?

(Thereafter, former President Trump continues explaining some of the issues with the election, legal scholar's opinions about Pence's ability to not certify the results from certain States and States legislatures that did not approve election changes).

The Federalist article cited above includes the audio of the interview and the transcript from the *Axios* article cited above.

As most of my readers know, I am an attorney with a civil practice. I routinely question witnesses in interviews, during depositions and at trial. (A deposition is a question-and-answer session where lawyers ask questions of a witness who is under oath. A recording or other record is made of the session and the questions and answers are typed up into a booklet type format.) A couple of issues arising in depositions in civil litigation will inform readers of the flaws with this interview and Fake News Media's arguments in this instance.

1. Jonathan Karl asked two questions at the same time in the snippet of the interview made public. Those are the questions about the safety of VP Pence. (Which I will refer to as the "Pence Safety Questions.") (The questions asked were, to summarized, "were you worried" about him - Mike Pence – and

"were you worried about his safety?")

2. President Trump clearly started to elaborate on another line of thought (and may have been answering a previous question) after he answered the "Pence Safety Questions" when he says, "But, but, no, I think —-," then his next words are "He could have" which is clearly a reference to VP Pence and "well people were very angry" which clearly (a) departed from the "He could have" line of thought and (b) was in response to Karl's statement (non-question) about "terrible" chants (before the "hang Mike Pence" observation is made).

3. We don't know if President Trump reverted, with his references to "But, but, no, I think —-" and "He could have . . .," to answering a previous question because we don't have the transcript. (This writer hunted high and low for the complete transcript of the 90 minute interview but could not find it.) Witnesses will routinely revert to answering an earlier question, particularly if the current question leads them away from a topic they were not ready to move on from.

4. Jonathan Karl and President Trump engage in what is known as "cross talk" during the exchange when Karl mentioned "hang Mike Pence." In other words, they both spoke at the same time. It is not even clear if Trump heard what Karl said from the audio.

First of all, these questions are being asked by a journalist, Jonathan Karl, who is not a lawyer. Karl asks two questions (at the same time) in the 36 second snippet of the interview. Those questions are:

Were you worried about him during that siege? Were you worried about his safety?

(A better question would have been "Where you worried about Vice President Pence's safety during the protests?" As it is readily apparent from President Trump's answer that is the question he answered when he said he was not worried about Pence because Pence was in "very good shape.")

After President Trump answers the question about Pence's safety he begins expressing another thought and says, "But, but, no, I think —-" We DON'T know here if President Trump is answering a question that was asked BEFORE the "Pence Safety Questions" because we don't have the transcript or the rest of the recording.

Then there is actually not another question asked by Jonathan Karl. Karl goes on with lamentations about the chants, saying "you heard those chants – that was terrible," and President Trump continues on his other thought and then interrupts that thought to observe people were very angry, saying "He could have – well the people were very angry" and then goes on to (1) either continue on the original line of thought or, arguably, (2) explain why people were angry.

President Trump was not asked a question about "hang Mike Pence." He heard Jonathan Karl's observation about the terrible chants after President Trump already expressed his understanding that VP Pence was safe.

Trump interrupts the thoughts he expressed to say the people were angry. That is the only defense he offered of the crowd and that was before Jonathan Karl made his statement (again without asking a question) about "hang Mike Pence."

Commentary: If the complete transcript of this interview is ever made public, I expect to we will learn President Trump was actually answering a previous question after he answered the "Pence Safety Questions." If one removes all of the "chant" observations by Jonathan Karl from this transcript and the single direct reference by President Trump to the chanting (that is the "well people were very angry" statement), here is what you get:

Question:

"Were you worried about him during that siege? Were you worried about his safety?"

Donald Trump:

"No, I thought he was well protected and I had heard he was in good shape. No. Because I had heard he was in very good shape.

But, but, no, I think—He could have, because it's - common sense Jon. It's common sense that you are supposed to protect. How can you – if you know a vote is fraudulent right? How can you pass on a fraudulent vote to Congress? How can you do that? And I'm telling you: 50/50, it's right down the middle for the top constitutional scholars when I speak to them. Anybody I spoke to – almost all of them at least pretty much agree, and some very much agree with me—because he's passing on a vote . . ."

That makes a lot more sense than the disjointed, cross-talking, interjected non-question lamentations the Fake News Media seized on. When the transcript is viewed in this manner it becomes abundantly clear the only defense of the crowd Trump made was to note they were "very angry" and that was before Jonathan Karl uttered a word about "hang Mike Pence."

This entire event underscores why attorneys are trained to ask questions in depositions and at trial and why an attorney who makes speeches, observations and expresses platitudes while examining witnesses in depositions or at trial will be met with objections. Demanding journalists question the subjects of their interviews with the skill and precision of an attorney examining a witness may be too much to ask, but the inartful way most journalists question their subjects is unfair to the people being interviewed

Nevertheless, at the absolute worst, one might plausibly claim President Trump did not condemn the chants from the crowd about "hanging" Mike Pence. Reporting on that accurately, however, would require one to note the cross talk at the precise moment when Jonathan Karl mentioned the "hang Mike Pence" issue and to note President Trump may not have even registered the comment due to the poor questioning. At the very least, before condemning President Trump, or anyone else for that matter, over an issue like this, one should at least have a direct question to answer. Donald Trump will never get that type of fair treatment from Fake News Media. You can take that to the bank.

17

TRUMP CANCELED THE WHITE HOUSE COMMENT LINE?

No, that was the Obama Administration.

Background: This Fake News story is about the White House Comment Line. Some readers may be unfamiliar with the White House Comment Line, so background may prove informative. As you undoubtedly know the White House is the official residence (Executive Mansion) of the President of the United States. (*The White House Historical Association* is a non-profit, private organization founded in 1961 to protect and preserve the history of the White House. Their website, *whitehousehistory.org*, is a terrific resource for those interested in the history of the White House.) For many years, a phone line to the White House has been dedicated for people to call and leave comments, notes or complaints. That line is known as the "White House Comment Line." For those interested in more background, a good article on the history of phone lines at the White House was published by *The Week*. See "*Who answers the White House phone, anyway?*" January 8, 2015, *theweek.com*. This next story deals with an interruption in the White House Comment Line's service in early 2017.

THE FAKE NEWS

Shortly after the inauguration in 2017, the Trump Administration shut down the White House Comment Line and the White House switchboard to prevent people from calling in and complaining about his Presidency.

Who Pushed the Fake News?

Addicting Info was one of the leading promoters of this piece of Fake News with its article, "*Trump Bans the Public From Calling The White House To Comment or Protest,*" published on January 23, 2107, only three days after President Trump's inauguration. (See Archive.today since the original article is no longer available.)

Common Dreams followed up with a similar story one week later on January 30, 2017, see *commondreams.org*:

Trump Shut Down White House Comment Line, So This Tool Lets You Call One of His Businesses to Complain

In an article also published on January 23, 2017, *The Washingtonian* also claimed the White House switchboard was closed. See *Washingtonian.com*. In fact, only the White House Comment Line was closed. (The White House switchboard literally consists of switchboard operators who transfer calls. *The White House Historical Association* has a webpage with a photo of the White House switchboard and switchboard operators with a brief explanation of the original installation of the switchboard in 1963. See *whitehousehistory.org*. *The New York Times* published an article in 1983 about the White House switchboard providing some background on the switchboard. See *The New York Times*, "*Whitehouse; A Switchboard That Is Justly Fabled,*" March 14, 1983, *nytimes.com*.) *The Washingtonian* corrected the article shortly after it was published. The correction at the end of the article reflects that and the headline reflects the story was updated. The original version of the headline is no longer available.

THE TRUTH

The Obama Administration shut down the White House Comment Line in early January 2017, before President Trump was inaugurated and before the Trump Administration started.

The Washington Times published an article on January 14, 2017, entitled "*White House Shuts Down Call Line,*" *washingtontimes.com*, outlining how the Obama Administration shut down the White House Comment Line and noted the Comment Line "apparently hasn't been operational for weeks."

Donald J. Trump was inaugurated as President of the United States on January 20, 2017. See *History.com*, "*Donald Trump is inaugurated,*" January 20, 2017. Therefore, the White House Comment Line was shut down by the Obama Administration.

Even *Snopes* rated the claim that "President Trump's administration shut down the White House phone comment line" as "mostly false." See *snopes.com*, "*Did President Trump Shut Down the White House Phone-In Comment Line?*" January 24, 2017.

Shortly after taking office, President Trump's administration reinstated the White House Comment Line. See *The Washington Times*, "*Donald Trump reopens White House comment line,*" February 16, 2017 *washingtontimes.com*.

Commentary: This particular story may not seem that significant. The story is included in this book because it illustrates a recurring theme of the Fake News Media throughout President Trump's term of office, i.e., how President Trump would get blamed for, or criticized for, actions actually taken by President

Obama, the Obama Administration or even previous administrations. More illustrations of this theme are found in Volumes Two and Three of this book series. Suffice it to say, if President Obama or his Administration did it, the Fake News Media would rarely say a word. They would, however, savage President Trump for things he did not do at all or for continuing the policies of previous administrations. The double-standard applied by the Fake News Media in this regard is pure Fake News.

18

HUNTER BIDEN LAPTOP STORY IS "RUSSIAN DISINFORMATION?"

No, the story is true.

Background: This particular Fake News story is not directly about Donald J. Trump himself and for that reason alone, I considered omitting it from this book. The "Hunter Biden Laptop" Fake News and the active suppression of the truth about the story, however, were used to help put Joe Biden in the White House. Thus, this particular piece of Fake News is as much about Donald J. Trump as one may get without the story actually being about him. I decided, therefore, to include the story in this book. Some background about the "Hunter Biden laptop" story is in order before getting to the merits of this Chapter's Fake News.

Hunter Biden, who was born in 1970, is the second son of President Joseph Biden. Hunter Biden has a long history of, shall we say, questionable business dealings, particularly overseas, where he appears to have cashed in on his father's political connections. An article by Vox, *"How much legal jeopardy is Hunter Biden in?"* April 11, 2022, *vox.com*, provides a good history of some of Hunter Biden's business deals. Of particular interest was Hunter Biden's appointment to the board of a Ukrainian energy company, Burisma, in May 2014, during his father's second term as Vice President and at the time then VP Biden was the "public face" of the Obama Administration's Ukraine policies. See The United States Senate Committee on Homeland Security and Governmental Affairs Report, "*Hunter Biden, Burisma and Corruption: The Impact on U.S. Government Policy and Related Concerns,*" September 2020. (Hereinafter, "Senate Report.") Interestingly enough, Hunter Biden reportedly had no experience in the energy industry at the time of this lucrative appointment. The money paid by Burisma alone to Hunter Biden (through LLCs owned or controlled by Biden) totals several million dollars. See *Senate Report,* pg. 67.

Importantly, at the time of Hunter Biden's appointment to the Burisma board in 2014, one of the owners of the company, a Ukrainian oligarch named Mykola Zlochevsky, was the subject of a corruption investigation by the Ukraine's Prosecutor General Office. To try to stop the investigation, Zlochevsky reportedly paid a $7,000,000.00 bribe to the Ukrainian Prosecutor General, all while Hunter Biden served on the Burisma board. See *Senate Report,* pg. 30.

The investigation into the Ukrainian oligarch was inherited (after the alleged bribe) by a new Prosecutor General, Viktor Shokin. In 2016, Viktor Shokin was fired at least in part at the insistence of then Vice President Joe Biden. See *Senate Report,* pgs. 8-9. This is the Ukrainian prosecutor Joe Biden, in 2018, boasted about strong-arming the Ukrainians into dismissing. See *Wall Street Journal Video,* "*WSJ Opinion: Hits and Misses of the Week,*" April 10, 2022, *wsj.com.* For his part, the Prosecutor General, Viktor Shokin, claims he was fired because U.S. VP Joe Biden was unhappy about Shokin's unwillingness to close the Burisma investigations. See *The Hill,* "*Solomon: These once-secret memos cast doubt on Joe Biden's Ukraine story,*" September 16, 2019, *thehill.com.* In 2020, a Ukrainian Court ordered an investigation into whether pressure from U.S. VP Joe Biden led to the dismissal of the Ukrainian Prosecutor General. See *The Washington Post,* "*Ukraine court forces probe into Biden role in firing of prosecutor Viktor Shokin*," February 27, 2020, *washingtonpost.com*.

(President Trump's discussion with Ukrainian President Volodymyr Zelensky on July 25, 2019, wherein President Trump mentioned the obvious conflicts-of-interest involved with then Vice President Biden's efforts to get the Ukrainian Prosecutor General fired and the need for the Ukraine to investigate the Bidens is what lead to the Democrats first ridiculous impeachment of President Trump. *The Federalist* ran a good article explaining this lunacy on February 10, 2021. See "*Hiding Biden: How Democrats And Media Crafted The First Impeachment to Help Defeat Trump in 2020*," *thefederalist.com*.)

But there is quite a bit more to Hunter Biden's shady dealings. Hunter Biden received over $3,000,000.00 from the wife of the former Mayor of Moscow (Russia), as well as millions of dollars from purported Chinese communists and others (some of whom are the subject of criminal investigations). See *Senate Report*, pgs. 65–85.

Also, for several months while he was on the Burisma board, Hunter Biden was protected by the United States Secret Service. See *Senate Report*, pg. 31.

To be polite, some of Hunter Biden's business dealings are questionable to say the least.

Then Candidate Biden claims ignorance about son's business dealings

In what appears to be an effort to insulate himself from the political liability posed by his son, Joe Biden claimed in 2019 that he never talked to his son Hunter about overseas business dealings. See *USA Today*, "*Biden: I never talked to son Hunter about overseas business dealings*," September 21, 2019, *usatoday.com*. Since taking office, President Biden continues to insist he never talked to Hunter Biden about Hunter Biden's foreign business interests. See *The New York Post*, "*Joe Biden sticking to claim he and Hunter Biden never talked about foreign business: Psaki*," April 5, 2022, *nypost.com*.

In October 2020, only weeks before the 2020 Presidential Election, *The New York Post* published a story about emails from a laptop belonging to Hunter Biden that confirmed Joe Biden not only knew about his son, Hunter's, business deals, but even met with a Burisma top executive, Vadym Pozharskyi, in 2015. See *The New York Post, "Smoking-gun email reveals how Hunter Biden introduced Ukrainian businessman to VP dad," October 14, 2020, nypost.com.*

This story and the series of stories it spawned are commonly referred to as the "Hunter Biden laptop" stories. The emails and other data were found on a laptop belonging to Hunter Biden which was dropped off at a computer repair shop in Delaware in April 2019. *The New York Post* story is the subject of this Chapter.

THE FAKE NEWS

The Hunter Biden laptop story is Russian disinformation.

Who Pushed the Fake News?

Politico led the charge with its story on October 19, 2020, a few days after *The New York Post* story ran, by publishing a letter signed by over 50 senior intelligence officials claiming the story had "all the classic earmarks of a Russian information operation." See *politico.com:*

Hunter Biden story is Russian disinfo, dozens of former intel officials say

The letter signed by the 50 plus intelligence officials was entitled, *Public Statement on the Hunter Biden Emails.* The letter suggested, without offering any evidence at all, the emails could have been hacked and manipulated.

Of course, *CNN* had to spring to the Biden's aid with print articles and broadcasts. On Sunday, October 18, 2020, *CNN* Chief Media Correspondent Brian Stelter addressed the Hunter Biden laptop story on his show, "*Reliable Sources*" (the irony of this Fake News Media heavyweight, *CNN*, and its chief "spin doctor," Stelter, labeling the show "Reliable Sources" is hard to bear). Stelter claimed the story was a "manufactured scandal" from the "right wing media machine," among other things:

The anatomy of the New York Post's dubious Hunter Biden story

U.S. Representative Adam Schiff, a California Democrat who serves on the United States House of Representatives Permanent Select Committee on Intelligence went on *The Situation Room* with Wolf Blitzer on *CNN* on October 16, 2020, and claimed ". . . we know this whole smear on Joe Biden comes from the Kremlin . . .," referencing the Hunter Biden laptop story. This broadcast may be found on *The Situation Room's* Twitter™ feed from October 16, 2020. (Readers will recall from previous Chapters, Rep. Schiff is the same guy who presented the altered, revised text from another lawmaker to former White House Chief of Staff Mark Meadows at a January 6 committee hearing and who fabricated quotes from President Trump during the First Impeachment trial. Keep his name in your mind if you do not know him already. He will pop up again. This guy takes spreading misinformation to the level of an art form.)

USA Today reported on October 17, 2020 that the FBI was investigating the potential for the laptop to be a "Russian disinformation campaign" and called *The New York Post* a "tabloid" that got a "trove of data on Hunter Biden."

A tabloid got a trove of data on Hunter Biden from Rudy Giuliani. Now, the FBI is probing a possible disinformation campaign.

Then Democrat Presidential Nominee Joe Biden called the story Russian disinformation believed only by Rudy Giuliani and President Trump during the last Presidential Debate in October 2020. See *Variety*, *"Joe Biden Accuses Trump of Using Russian 'Plant' in Final Debate,"* October 22, 2020, *variety.com.*

Twitter™ locked *The New York Post* out of its account for two weeks due to the story and blocked links to the story to prevent the story from being shared on the social media platform. See *Business Insider*, *"Jack Dorsey says the New York Post Twitter account will remain locked until it deletes the original tweet featuring its Hunter Biden story,"* October 28, 2020, *businessinsider.com.*

Facebook™ limited the distribution of the story on its platform. *See The New York Post*, *"Facebook limits spread of The Post's Hunter Biden expose'"* October 14, 2020, *nypost.com.*

Virtually every Fake News Media outlet in existence called into question the Hunter Biden laptop story, but the articles and broadcasts cited above are good illustrations.

THE TRUTH

The Hunter Biden laptop and *The New York Post* story were not Russian disinformation. The story is true.

Let's start with the letter from the 50 plus senior intelligence officials, the *Public Statement on the Hunter Biden Emails*. The letter actually does not claim the emails from the laptop are disinformation. In relevant part, the letter reads that the story:

". . . has all the classic earmarks of a Russian *information* operation. (Emphasis added) . . .

We want to emphasize we do not know if the emails . . . are genuine or not and that we do not have evidence of Russian involvement – just that our experience makes us deeply suspicious that the Russian government played a significant role in this case."

In an interview after the Presidential Election, one of the drafters of the Intelligence Letter, Marc Polymeropoulos, a former CIA officer, stated the letter was not intended to question the authenticity of the Hunter laptop emails and that the letter referenced the potential for the emails to be a " . . . Russian information operation, it's not disinformation." See *Hernando Sun*, "*Fact Check: 2020 Lie of the Year*," January 8, 2021, *hernandosun.com*.

On October 19, 2020, the Director of National Intelligence John Ratcliffe confirmed the Hunter Biden laptop/emails were "NOT part of some Russian disinformation campaign." (Emphasis added.) See *The New York Post*, *nypost.com*:

DNI John Ratcliffe says info on Hunter Biden laptop isn't Russian disinformation

The Federal Bureau of Investigation and the United States Department of Justice confirmed the Hunter Biden laptop was not part of any Russian disinformation campaign. See *Washington Examiner*, October 20, 2020, *washingtonexaminer.com*:

FBI and DOJ do not believe Hunter Biden laptop part of Russian disinformation campaign

In interviews in March 2022, former Attorney General of the United States William Barr slammed Joe Biden for lying about Hunter's laptop. Barr stated:

"I was very disturbed during the debate when candidate Biden lied to the American people about the laptop. . . he suggested it was Russian disinformation and pointed to the letter written by some intelligence people that was baseless – which he knew was a lie."

See *Fox News*, March 21, 2022, *foxnews.com*:

Bill Barr says Joe Biden lied to Americans about Hunter Biden laptop: 'I was very disturbed'

The former Attorney General went on to say the lies about the laptop being "Russian disinformation" bordered on "election interference" with respect to the 2020 Presidential Election. See *Daily Mail*, "*Bill Barr slams Biden for 'lying' about that his son Hunter's laptop was 'Russian disinformation' and says his claims were verging on 'election interference,*" March 21, 2022, *dailymail.co.uk*.

In 2022, *The New York Times* finally acknowledged the Hunter Biden laptop emails were authentic in an article published on March 16, 2022. *Fox News* lampooned *The New York Times* the following day for its untimely confirmation and for "dismissing" the laptop for the previous two years:

New York Times finally confirms Hunter Biden's laptop after dismissing it amid 2020 campaign

As *The Wall Street Journal* reported in an article by the WSJ Editorial Board on September 24, 2021, *wsj.com*, that even *Politico* confirmed the authenticity of the laptop and emails:

Vindication Over Hunter's Emails
Politico confirms the New York Post story the Bidens never denied.

The Washington Post got around to confirming the authenticity of the Hunter Biden laptop emails (or at least the ones at issue) on March 30, 2022. See *"Here's how The Post analyzed Hunter Biden's laptop," washingtonpost.com.*

The bottom line is the Hunter Biden laptop emails were not Russian misinformation at all. That was actually clear shortly after the story came out, as the citations above reflect. The emails exposed by *The New York Post* article have been verified by virtually everyone at this point.

Despite these facts, the 51 lying intelligence experts still refuse to apologize for the misinformation in their letter. We know, because *The New York Post* reached out to each one of them and wrote about it on March 18, 2022, see *nypost.com*:

Spies who lie: 51 'intelligence' experts refuse to apologize for discrediting true Hunter Biden story

Commentary: According to a Media Research Center poll, 16% of Biden voters would have voted differently if the Hunter Biden laptop story had not been suppressed by Fake News Media and Big Tech. See *The Post Millennial*, *"Flashback: 16% of Biden voters would have voted differently if Hunter Biden laptop story was not suppressed by media, big tech,"* March 17, 2022, *thepostmillennial.com.* In another survey by Rasmussen Reports, 66% of Americans say the Hunter Biden laptop is an "important story." See *The New York Post*, *"Two-thirds of Americans say Hunter Biden laptop "important" story: poll,"* March 25, 2022, *nypost.com.* Thus, the Hunter Biden laptop story, had it been properly reported on, could have (and likely would have) changed the outcome of the 2020 Presidential Election. And the laptop was just the beginning. Imagine if the press reported on Hunter Biden's business partner, Tony Bobulinski, who confirmed Joe Biden is the "big guy" referenced in the emails who got a 10% cut of the some of Hunter's business deals. See *The Wall Street Journal*, *"The Biden 'Family Legacy,"* October 22, 2020, *wsj.com* and *Daily Mail*, *"Exclusive: Psaki in denial: Hunter's emails reveal 'Big Guy' Joe Biden was to get 10% stake in Chinese oil deal, dined with Hunter's shady business partners when he was VP, shared a bank account with his son and flew associate to Mexico on Air Force 2,"* April 8, 2022, *dailymail.co.uk.*

If this laptop belonged to Donald Trump, Jr., can you imagine the Fake News Media hyperventilating as it repeated these stories relentlessly? Do you think those 51 "intelligence experts" would have signed a letter casting any doubt on the story? Of course not.

Imagine if one of President Trump's children was the focus of investigations for Federal tax fraud, money laundering and acting as an unregistered foreign agent? Those are the precise issues for which Hunter Biden is being investigated. See *Vox*, *"How much legal jeopardy is Hunter Biden in?"* April 11, 2022, *vox.com.* And just imagine if President Trump were implicated in *any* of the questionable dealings involving President Joe Biden outlined in the *Daily Mail* article cited in the previous paragraph. The Democrat politicians and Fake News Media would be screaming from the roof tops day and night for impeachment.

The fact is 51 "intelligence experts" signed off on a letter claiming, based only on experience and without any evidence, that the Hunter Biden laptop story was a "Russian *information* operation" (not *disinformation* operation) intended to influence our election. They did this likely knowing full well the Fake News Media would transform their claim from a Russian *information* operation into a Russian *disinformation* operation. The truth is the only misinformation spread with the intent to influence our 2020 Presidential Election, with respect to the Hunter Biden laptop, was spread by the Fake News Media and *American former intelligence officials in their effort to put Biden in the White House.* That ought to shock (and frighten) everyone. At least now you know the truth.

19

NO ONE PROFITED LIKE TRUMP AFTER LEAVING OFFICE?

Except for the Clintons and Obamas

THE FAKE NEWS

Since the end of his Presidency, Donald J. Trump is profiting from his time in office in an unprecedented fashion.

Who Pushed the Fake News?

The New York Times in an article published on February 12, 2022, *nytimes.com*:

Selling Trump: A Profitable Post-Presidency Like No Other

The NYT article starts with a story about former President Trump boarding the private plane of some business "magnates" and flying to Naples, Florida where he attends a party with people who paid somewhere between $10,000 to $30,000.00 for the privilege. The NYT claimed the event "had all the trappings" of a political fundraiser, but the money went "straight" into Trump's pocket, according to an anonymous source, labeled "a person familiar with the arrangement." (After all, the NYT would not want to publish Fake News story about Donald J. Trump without referencing at least one anonymous source.)

The article goes on to delineate multiple different endeavors undertaken by former President Trump to make money since leaving office, including an arena tour with former Fox News host Bill O'Reilly, publishing a coffee-table book and an online Trump store.

The NYT makes passing mention of efforts of former Presidents Clinton, Obama and George W. Bush to make money after leaving office, but claims ". . . no former president has been more determined to meld his business interests – from chocolate bars to real estate to a tech start-up —with a political operation and capitalize on that for personal gain."

The NYT threw in some swipes about the former First Lady Melania Trump's efforts to sell some art pieces and questioned whether some of her upcoming charity work is for properly permitted charitable organizations.

The NYT even threw in that some "watchdogs" were worried during his Presidency that President Trump might be "selling access" and somehow these groups "remain concerned."

THE TRUTH

The fact is former Presidents Bill Clinton, Barack Obama and (to a lesser extent) George W. Bush all cashed in handsomely on their former office. No First Lady ever cashed in on her fame like Hillary Clinton. Furthermore, the claim made by *The New York Times* that no other president "melded" his businesses with political operations is more than a little misleading, since former Presidents Bill Clinton and Barack Obama had no businesses before assuming political office.

Simply stated, the Clintons and the Obamas monetized their time in office as much, or more, than anyone else. Let's take a look at the details.

After leaving office in 2001 through the spring of 2015, according to *CNN*, former President Bill Clinton and former First Lady Hillary Clinton were paid over $153,000,000.00 for speeches. See *CNN*, February 6, 2016, *cnn.com*:

$153 million in Bill and Hillary Clinton speaking fees, documented

After resigning her position as Secretary of State in the Obama Administration, former First Lady Hillary Clinton raked in $22,000,000.00 in speaking fees, according to *U.S. News & World Report*. In fact, some of the speaking fees were paid apparently by groups with Federal contracts or that lobbied the Clinton State Department. See *U.S. News & World Report*, April 22, 2016, *usnews.com*:

Here's Who Paid Hillary Clinton $22 Million in Speaking Fees

Former President Clinton, for his part, charges as much as $500,000.00 to $750,000.00 for speeches. See *New York Daily News*, "*Bill Clinton is paid $500,000 speaking advance for 45 minute speech, earning $11,100 per minute,*" June 3, 2013, *nydailynews.com* and *Los Angeles Times*, "*Behind a Bill Clinton speaking engagement: A $1,400 hotel phone bill and $700 dinner for two,*" July 11, 2016, *latimes.com*.

In addition, through a series of deals, including book deals, consulting with private companies and their lucrative speaking engagement deals, the Clintons actually made $240,000,000.00 from 2001 to 2016. See *Forbes Magazine*, November 8, 2016, *forbes.com*:

How Bill And Hillary Clinton Made $240 Million In The Last 15 Years

The revenue brought in by The Clinton Foundation, however, makes the amounts paid to former President Bill Clinton and former First Lady Hillary Clinton seem quite small. According to an investigation by *The Washington Post* in 2015, The Clinton Foundation raised nearly $2,000,000,000.00 (that is right, nearly $2 billion) from 2001 to 2015, including millions of dollars "from seven foreign governments during Hillary Rodham Clinton's tenure as secretary of state." See *The Washington Post*, "*Foreign governments gave millions to foundation while Clinton was at State Dept.*," February 25, 2015, *washingtonpost.com*.

And insofar as "selling access" is concerned, according to an analysis by *The New York Post* in 2016, *nypost.com*, the majority of Clinton Foundation mega-donors obtained special access to Hillary Clinton when she was secretary of state:

Majority of Clinton Foundation donors got special access to Hillary

As for the Obamas, as of 2018, they were worth over $135,000,000.00, according to *The New York Post*, November 17, 2018, *nypost.com*:

The Obamas are 'Becoming' a billion-dollar brand

Plus, the Obamas reportedly cashed in on a $65,000,000.00 advance for their joint book rights. See *Vanity Fair*, *"Barack and Michelle Obama Land Reported $65 Million Book Deal,"* March 1, 2017, *vanityfair.com*.

In addition, the Obamas signed a lucrative deal with Netflix to produce original programming. See *Newsweek*, *"Obama Netflix: What the Former President and First Lady's Deal Is Worth and What They're Producing,"* September 17, 2019, *newsweek.com*. The precise amount of money paid by Netflix to the Obamas is elusive, but according to *CNN Money* the deal is "8 figures." See, *CNN Business*, *"Pacific * What Netflix paid for the Obamas,"* May 21, 2018, *money.cnn.com*.

And in 2019, the Obamas signed a deal with podcast giant Spotify to produce and host podcasts (though terms of the deal were not publicly released). See *The Hollywood Reporter*, *"Obamas Ink Deal With Spotify to Produce, Host Podcasts,"* June 6, 2019, *hollywoodreporter.com*.

When the high-dollar deal with Spotify petered out, the Obamas cashed in again, this time by signing a reported $20 million dollar deal with Amazon-owned platform Audible in June 2022 to apparently produce similar content to the Spotify deal. See *Daily Mail*, *"Barack and Michelle Obama's Amazon Audible deal is worth $20 MILLION and will feature them in eight episodes each, experts say - after they ditched Spotify amid fallout over exclusivity and how often they had to appear in shows,"* June 22, 2022, *dailymail.co.uk*.

Comparing to the Clintons and Obamas, former President George W. Bush charges a pedestrian $100,000.00 to $175,000.00 per appearance on the speaking circuit. See *Politico*, *"On talk circuit, George W. Bush makes millions, but few waves,"* June 8, 2015, *politico.com*. He was also paid a $7,000,000.00 advance for his book *Decision Points*, in 2010. See *Business Insider*, *"Hey*

Congress, Tax Bush's $7 Million Book Advance at 90%," March 19, 2009, *businessinsider.com.* Former President George W. Bush is not the Clintons or Obamas, but he has done well since leaving office.

In summary, the Clintons and Obamas elevated post-presidency money-making to an art form. For that, they get praised by the press. (Do you notice the different tone when the Obamas get a $65 million dollar book deal and a former Republican president gets a $7 million dollar book deal?) Former President Trump follows in their footsteps and gets lampooned by the press.

Commentary: Can you imagine the hue and cry from the Fake News Media if Donald J. Trump received a $65 million book advance? Or if President Trump formed a foundation and raked in billions of dollars while he held public office like Hillary Clinton did? The fact is the Clintons and Obamas made money like no one else since leaving office. President Trump may be creative, but for *The New York Times* to pretend Trump is more of a profiteer than the Clintons or Obamas is pure Fake News.

20

TRUMP AND DESANTIS ARE FEUDING?

Not really.

THE FAKE NEWS

Former President Trump and Florida Governor Ron DeSantis are feuding over who will lead the Republican Party.

Who Pushed the Fake News?

Once again, the purveyor of this Fake News is *The New York Times.* In an article published on January 16, 2022, *nytimes.com*, The NYT claimed:

Who Is King of Florida? Tensions Rise Between Trump and a Former Acolyte.

The article is replete with all of the hallmarks of typical NYT Fake News, including multiple anonymous "sources" who provide juicy details and purported quotes about former President Trump's complaints about the

Florida Governor, along with "insider" gossip and speculation.

The article starts by claiming former President Trump has been "grumbling quietly to friends and visitors" about the Florida Governor "for months."

After rambling on for paragraphs about the supposed origins and nature of the alleged dispute, the article then claims Gov. DeSantis told ". . . friends he believes Mr. Trump's expectation that he bend the knee is asking too much."

The article claims former President Trump asked several "associates and advisors, who spoke on the condition of anonymity" that "I wonder why the guy won't say he won't run against me."

The NYT goes on to claim some comments former President Trump made about politicians who won't comment on their COVID booster status were directed at Governor DeSantis, then the article claims Governor DeSantis "responded" by referencing his opposition to the original COVID lockdowns.

Axios ran an article of its own, also on January 16, 2022, *axios.com*:

Trump dogs "dull" DeSantis ahead of potential 2024 matchup

The *Axios* article claims former President Trump "trashes" Governor DeSantis in private calling the Governor an "ingrate" with a "dull personality." The article is based on, you guessed it, an anonymous source "who recently spoke to Trump about Desantis."

Axios then claims a "second source who's discussed DeSantis with Trump" claims former President Trump's unhappiness stems from the Governor's unwillingness to say the Governor won't run for President in 2024. *Axios* then claims, as the NYT did in its article on the subject, that former President Trump's comment about politicians who won't comment on their COVID booster status was directed at Gov. DeSantis.

These articles read more like tabloid gossip than actual journalism, but that is apparently what passes for journalism at *The New York Times* and *Axios* these days.

THE TRUTH

Former President Trump and Florida Governor Ron DeSantis both confirm these tabloid-style rumors are Fake News.

Within days of these reports, on January 20, 2022, *The New York Post* ran an article wherein President Trump addressed the rumors, *nypost.com*:

Trump says he has 'very good relationship' with DeSantis amid rumors of feud

The article quotes former President Trump as stating he has "a very good relationship with him" (Governor DeSantis) and that Trump is ". . . very supportive of him and I continue to be" and that he thinks the Florida Governor is ". . . good, I think he's very good."

For his part, in an interview with *Fox News*, *foxnews.com*, on February 8, 2022, Governor DeSantis addressed the rumors:

DeSantis insists narrative of Trump rivalry is 'total bunk': He's 'a friend of mine'

Governor DeSantis went on to state former President Trump wants to see Republicans "doing well," and that he thinks the media stories are "total bunk" and that those in the media are ". . . just making it up." The Governor also went on to defend the former president from the efforts of the January 6th Committee and Rep. Liz Cheney whom the Governor characterized as having a "vendetta" against Donald Trump.

Does this sound like two politicians who are feuding? Not hardly. Particularly, given the fact the former president is more than willing to call out any Republican politician with whom he has an actual dispute or disagreement. At one time or other, candidate Trump, President Trump and former President Trump had, or has, actual feuds with U.S. Senators Lindsay Graham (R-SC) and Ted Cruz (R-TX)(see, *Today, "Lindsay Graham criticizes Donald Trump, Ted Cruz wife feud: 'Knock this crap off,'"* March 24, 2016, *today.com*), Mitch McConnell (R-KY) (see, *Newsweek, "Trump Calls McConnell 'Best Thing That Ever Happened' to Democrats as Feud Escalates,"* December 18, 2021, *newsweek.com*), Lisa Murkowski (R-AK)(see *Politico, "Trump vows to campaign against 'disloyal' Murkowski,"* March 6, 2021, politico.com), Ben Sasse (R-NE)(see *USA Today, 'Not going to waste a single minute on tweets': GOP Sen. Sasse pushes back after Trump attacks,"* October 17, 2020, *usatoday.com*), former U.S. Senator John McCain (R-AZ)(see *AZ Central, "The John McCain-Donald Trump feud,"* March 20, 2019, *azcentral.com*), and former Speaker of the United States House of Representatives Paul Ryan (see *Axios, "Trump: People like Paul Ryan almost killed the Republican Party,"* July 13, 2019, *axios.com*), to name a few.

A couple of anonymous gossipers who supposedly talked to *The New York Times* and *Axios* is nowhere near enough to confirm an actual feud between

Donald J. Trump and anyone, let alone a friend and ally like Florida Governor Ron DeSantis.

Commentary: If President Trump had an actual dispute or problem with Governor Ron DeSantis he would say so. Since Donald Trump announced his run for office in 2015, he demonstrated a willingness to call out and mix it up with any politician in the GOP he became at odds with. Some of these feuds are legendary, such as his feud with former Senator John McCain. For entertainment, just go back and look at some of the biting criticism President Trump had for Sen. McCain (and vice versa). Why would Donald Trump suddenly fear criticizing Governor DeSantis, if he had any such criticism to levy?

Furthermore, what kind of Republican "friend" or "associate" of President Trump or Governor DeSantis would run to *The New York Times* or *Axios* to report the private conversations of either man? Conservatives are the only people who would care about such a feud and conservatives are instantly suspicious of either of these Fake News Media heavyweights. Lastly, these stories are just further proof of the depths to which the Fake News Media sunk. How in the world is gossip like this newsworthy? What kind of journalist would write these stories and what kind of publication would print these stories in the first place? The Fake News Media gets more ridiculous by the day.

21

TRUMPS CLAIMS ABOUT WINDMILLS ARE WRONG?

No, President Trump's claims were on the money.

THE FAKE NEWS

During the climate change/environmental portion of the second Presidential Debate on October 22, 2020, President Trump's claims that windmill farms kill birds, are extremely expensive and produce power intermittently were disingenuous, dishonest and wrong.

Who Pushed the Fake News?

Vox peddled this nonsense the following day, October 23, 2020, with this article on *vox.com*:

Donald Trump's issue with windmills might not be about birds

The article claimed President Trump's issues with windmills were pretextual, disingenuous or dishonest. The article quoted President Trump as stating "I know more about wind than you do. It's extremely expensive. Kills all the birds. It's very intermittent."

The article called into question President Trump's accuracy and sincerity by noting cats kill more birds than anything else, an average of 2.4 billion per year, citing the report by the United States Fish and Wildlife Service, entitled "*Threats to Birds*" (citing data from 2017).

Vox claimed if President Trump was truly interested in saving the lives of birds, he would take some sort of action about the cat problem. *Vox* characterized the President's claims as "silliness."

THE TRUTH

President Trump made several claims about wind energy in that second Presidential Debate. He was correct (though he did embellish the bird killing issue by saying wind energy/windmill farms "kills all the birds").

Let us begin by reviewing what President Trump actually said about wind energy and windmills in that debate:

"We are energy independent for first time. We don't need all of these countries that we had to fight war over because we needed their energy. We are energy independent. I know more about wind than you do. It's extremely expensive. Kills all the birds. It's very intermittent. It's got a lot of problems and they happen to make the windmills in both Germany and China and the fumes coming up, if you're a believer in carbon emission, the fumes coming up to make these massive windmills is more than anything that we're talking about with natural gas, which is very clear."

See the *Second Debate Transcript* published at *Rev.com* (the relevant comments are made at the 1 hour, 18 minute, 56 second mark in the transcript).

What claims did President Trump make about windmills and wind energy? He claimed:

1. Windmills or wind energy is "extremely expensive." (We know President Trump referred here to windmills, because his next words were about killing birds, then about intermittency, then about where "windmills" are made. Furthermore, then candidate Biden had just talked about "windmills.")
2. It "kills all the birds,"
3. It "is very intermittent,"
4. Windmills are made in Germany and China, and
5. The fumes generated while making massive windmills are more than what is made by natural gas.

Reviewing these claims, we find:

1. Windmills are "extremely expensive." They are. Wind turbines cost an average of $1.3 million per megawatt (MW) of nameplate capacity installed. Most commercial wind turbines have 2-3 MW capacity making the cost of each individual turbine from $2.6 million to nearly $4 million dollars. See *Weather Guard, "Wind Turbine Cost: How Much? Are They Worth It In 2022?"* December 20, 2021, *weatherguardwind.com* and *Wind Industry, "How much do wind turbines cost?" windustry.com.*

There are additional costs beyond just the original construction. The cost of the land is another factor. Also, once built, ongoing wind turbine maintenance costs are 1-2 cents per kilowatt-hour produced or roughly $42,000.00 to $48,000.00 per year, per turbine. See *Weather Guard, "Wind Turbine Cost: How Much? Are They Worth It In 2022?"* December 20, 2021, *weatherguardwind.com*

In addition, wind farms tend to be located in rural areas, thereby requiring the use of long transmission lines (resulting in the loss of energy) and extensive transmission line costs. See *Nuclear Newswire*, *"The economics of wind power,"* January 27, 2011, *ans.org*.

So, those wind farms you may have seen while driving down the Interstate in West Texas with hundreds of giant wind turbines? Those cost a *lot of money*.

President Trump was right, windmills and generating wind energy is extremely expensive.

2. Windmills or wind energy "kills all the birds." Okay, President Trump exaggerated here, but the issue is do windmills kill birds? Yes, they do.

According to a 2021 study of bird deaths caused by wind turbines by the *American Bird Conservancy* approximately 681,000 birds are killed annually by wind turbines in the United States. See *American Bird Conservancy*, *"How Many Birds Are Killed By Wind Turbines?"* January 26, 2021, *abcbirds.org*. (The U.S. Fish and Wildlife Service study cited in the *Vox* article put that number at approximately 234,000.) Some estimates of the bird kills from windmills are far, far higher. See *windmillskill.com*. (*Windmillskill.com* also includes articles outlining why the estimates of bird kills at wind farms are probably far lower than the true number. Reasons for the undercount include research parameters confined to a 200 foot radius around turbines when birds are often thrown much farther than that and USFW guidelines calling for searching small areas only every 30-90 days. See *windmillskill.com*.)

The *American Bird Conservancy* also published an article in March 2021 outlining how significant the threat posed by wind turbines is to birds and calling out the misleading nature of the comparison of wind turbine to cat deaths made by some (these same arguments were made by *Vox* in its attack piece on President Trump). See *American Bird Conservancy*, *"Are Wind Turbines A Significant Threat To Birds?"* March 2, 2021, *abcbirds.org*.

In April 2022, wind energy company ESI Energy Inc., pleaded guilty to killing over 150 eagles at its wind farms and paid an $8 million dollar fine. See *Smithsonian Magazine*, "*Wind Energy Company Pleads Guilty to Killing Eagles*," April 11, 2022, *smithsonianmag.com*.

The bottom line is windmills kill a lot of birds. Again, President Trump was right.

3. Windmills generate power intermittently (meaning, at irregular intervals, not steadily or continuously). Again, this is true. Wind energy is only generated when the wind is blowing and blowing from the right direction, with air at the right density and with sufficient force to activate turbines. As *Energy Education*, an educational project of the University of Calgary, confirms "Wind power is considered highly intermittent and non-dispatchable because it is a variable power source, meaning its electrical output depends on many factors, such as wind speed, air density, turbine characteristics and more." See *energyeducation.ca*, "*Intermittent electricity*." More authority for the intermittency of wind power could be cited, but this point is not debatable, since the wind is not always blowing, is not always blowing from the right direction, is not always blowing with sufficient force and is not always the right density.

4. Wind turbines are made in China and Germany. According to *Biz Vibe* in 2020, when President Trump made his statement about wind turbines being made in China and Germany, 8 of the 10 top wind turbine manufacturers in the world were located in China and Germany. See *Biz Vibe*, "*Global Wind Turbine Industry Factsheet 2022: Top 10 Largest Wind Turbine Manufacturers*," May 26, 2022, *blog.bizvibe.com*. 1 of the others was located in Denmark and 1 in the United States. Also in 2020, *REVE* (the Spanish initials for the *Wind Energy and Electric Vehicle Magazine*) confirmed China alone held 7 of the top 10 spots among wind turbine makers. See *REVE*, "*China takes up 7 spots among the world's top 10 wind turbine manufacturers for wind power*," March 13, 2021, *evwind.es*.

President Trump was right again.

5. Fumes generated during the manufacturing of the components of massive wind mill farms are greater than for extracting natural gas. President Trump appears to be right again. As *Carbon Market Watch* confirms the waste gases (fumes) from the manufacturing process for steel is worse for the climate than coal, let alone natural gas. Wind turbines are predominantly made of steel. See *Carbon Market Watch*, *"Waste gases from steel worse for the climate than coal,"* October 9, 2018, *carbonmarketwatch.com*.

Once again, President Trump appears to be correct. I say "appears to be" correct, because depending on what he meant in this part of his statement he could be wrong. In the last part of his statement about wind mills, President Trump mentioned "carbon emissions" and then mentioned the fumes from manufacturing windmill farms. *If President Trump meant natural gas extraction or production resulted in less carbon emissions than windmill farm manufacturing, then that statement would be incorrect.*

There is actually a tremendous amount of research about the total carbon footprint of wind energy (from manufacturing, to transport, construction, maintenance, etc...), and other forms of energy development. The science of determining this carbon footprint is known as "life cycle assessment." The carbon footprint of "massive windmills" is far, far less than generating natural gas energy. There are numerous comparative studies confirming this fact, but the study *"Life cycle costs and carbon emissions of wind power,"* by *Scotland's Centre of Expertise on Climate Change* from 2015, *climatexchange.org.uk*, is very well done and an easy read.

Nevertheless, the reference to "fumes" made by President Trump in this portion of his statement was probably a reference to the toxic fumes generated during the manufacturing process for steel wind turbines and those toxic emissions do appear worse than those generated during natural gas production. See *Carbon Market Watch*, *"Waste gases from steel worse for the climate than coal,*" October 9, 2018, *carbonmarketwatch.com.*

Commentary: Once again, President Trump spoke in a knowledgeable, informed manner about the issues with windmills, windfarms and wind energy, regardless of the tongue-in-cheek Fake News attacks from *Vox.* Wind energy is costly to generate and distribute. Wind only produces energy when the wind is dense enough, blows hard enough, from the right direction and turbines are well placed and in good working order. Further, the majority of wind turbines are made in China and/or Germany. President Trump was correct about all of the above. He was right about something else as well, namely, that he, Trump, knows more about wind energy than Joe Biden. That is probably what *Vox* hoped to obscure with this silly attack on Trump.

22

TRUMP STORMED OUT OF AN INTERVIEW WITH PIERS MORGAN?

No, he did not. The interview ended politely.

THE FAKE NEWS

Former President Donald Trump stormed out of an interview with Piers Morgan after Morgan pressed Trump about Trump's claims that the 2020 U.S. Presidential Election was stolen.

Who Pushed the Fake News?

Piers Morgan himself in an article for *The New York Post* on April 20, 2022, *nypost.com*:

How all hell broke loose after my fiery showdown with Trump over his stolen election claims

The interview was done for Piers Morgan's new show, *Piers Morgan Uncensored*, and the article written by Morgan claims former President Trump became incensed when Morgan challenged him about Trump's claims the election was stolen. Morgan claimed that Trump left the interview:

". . . abruptly jumping to his feet, looking hateful, and barking at the shocked crew to: 'TURN THE CAMERAS OFF.' Then he turned on his heel and sloped angrily through a side door loudly mutter 'so dishonest.'" See *PJ Media*, "*No, Trump Did Not 'Storm Off the Set' of Piers Morgan's Interview Show,*" April 21, 2022, *pjmedia.com.*

A 30 second promotional ad for the interview and Piers Morgan's new show uses edited clips from the interview to create the appearance that former President Trump stormed out of the interview before it was over. See *Hot Air*, "*So it looks like Piers Morgan misled everyone about Trump storming off of his show,*" April 21, 2022, *hotair.com* (the story includes a link to the video promo).

THE TRUTH

President Trump did not storm out of the interview. The interview ended with an exchange of pleasantries between Trump and Morgan. Furthermore, the interview was supposed to be 20 minutes, but President Trump stayed for over an hour's worth of questions. The comment from President Trump about turning off the cameras was after the friendly conclusion of the interview.

The reason we know all of this is President Trump's team recorded the interview and released the recording to the press. *NBC News* published an article about the issue on April 20, 2022, *nbcnews.com:*

TRUMP STORMED OUT OF AN INTERVIEW WITH PIERS MORGAN?

Trump releases audio that appears to refute claim he walked out of interview over 2020 questions

The former president's communications director released audio that shows reports that Trump had stormed off in response to questions about his election claims were inaccurate.

A *PJ Media* article from April 21, 2022, *pjmedia.com*, provides excerpts of the representations of Piers Morgan in his article, a link to the promotional add for Piers Morgan's new show (wherein the interview is edited and spliced to sensationalize the events) and a link to the audio from Trump's camp:

No, Trump Did Not 'Storm Off the Set' of Piers Morgan's Interview Show

The audio recording reflects Piers Morgan and President Trump exchanged pleasantries at the end of the interview with Piers Morgan stating "That was a great interview" and President Trump agreeing. Morgan then thanks President Trump for the interview.

Breitbart also published an article on April 20, 2022, about the "Deceptive Edits" used by Morgan. See "*Deceptive Edits: Audio Contradicts Piers Morgan, Shows He Warped Trump Interview Ending in Promo*," Breitbart.com. This article includes a link to the audio produced by the Trump camp.

When the second part of Morgan's interview with former President Trump aired on Tuesday, April 26, 2022, the video confirmed Trump did not storm out of the interview. See *The Independent, independent.co.uk*:

Piers Morgan reveals Trump did not storm out of interview as he attacks ex-president's 'incompetent' aide

<u>Commentary</u>: Fake News takes all forms. This particular piece of Fake News was made to promote Piers Morgan's new show and his interview with former President Trump. What better way to promote the show than by cleverly splicing parts of an interview that ran for over an hour to make it look as though Trump became angry and ended the interview early by walking off the set? The fact is the interview ended in a routine way with former President Trump and Piers Morgan thanking one another and laughing. Undoubtedly, there were some "fiery" moments in the interview (to borrow the characterization of Morgan), but that is apparently not sufficient to promote the show. Nevertheless, how can someone abruptly end an interview 45 minutes after the interview was supposed to be over? Why would anyone even try to claim someone "stormed off" the set of an interview that ran 45 minutes over its allotted time? Piers Morgan has always been a holier-than-thou know-it-all. This episode did not improve his image.

23

TRUMP SAID AMERICANS HAVE NO RIGHT TO PROTEST HIM?

No, he did not.

THE FAKE NEWS

In the spring of 2017, at the beginning of his Presidency, President Trump claimed Americans have no right to protest him.

Who Pushed the Fake News?

The website *Learn Progress* claimed, in an online article published on April 22, 2017, the Trump Administration argued in court that it was illegal for American citizens to protest him. See *Archive Today*. (The *Learn Progress* website, *learnprogress.org*, is apparently defunct. The website to *Archive.Today* which preserved the page at *https://archive.ph/ToPqd*.)

The article claimed the effort was one of President Trump's "most alarming moves yet," contending Trump is ". . . literally arguing in court that it's *illegal* for America citizens to protest against him at his campaign rallies." (Emphasis original.) The article went on to claim the President's efforts in this regard were "TYRANNY."

The article notes the issue arose in a suit filed by three people who disrupted a Trump rally in Louisville in 2016. *Learn Progress* claimed the President (who was then only a candidate for the office) incited violence against the individuals who disrupted the rally. *Learn Progress* took great issue with the legal arguments of President Trump's legal team in defense of the lawsuit.

THE TRUTH

President Trump's legal team did not argue Americans did not have the right to protest President Trump. Basically, President Trump's legal team argued Trump and Trump supporters had the right to lawfully assemble without unlawful interference and that then candidate Trump's speech was First Amendment Protected Speech. President Trump's legal team was correct. A link to the Trump legal team's brief may be found in an article by *Politico* published on April 20, 2017, *"Trump lawyer: 'No right' to protest at rallies,"* *politico.com.*

Even *Snopes* rated the claim made by *Learn Progress* as "mostly false." See *Snopes, "Did Trump Say Americans Had 'No Right' To Protest Against Him?"* May 9, 2017, *snopes.com.*

The case referenced by *Learn Progress* arose out of a 2016 Trump rally in Louisville, Kentucky. The name of the case was *Nwanguma vs. Trump.* The appellate opinion from the United States Court of Appeals for the Sixth Circuit is reported at 903 F. 3d 604 (6th Cir. 2018). The Court dismissed the claims against Donald J. Trump, finding Trump's speech was fully protected by the First Amendment.

In fact, the three clowns who disrupted and interfered with the Trump rally were in violation of the law. Kentucky Revised Statute §525.150 makes it a "Class B Misdemeanor" when a person ". . . with intent to prevent or disrupt a lawful meeting, procession or gathering . . .," and then ". . . does any act tending to obstruct or interfere with it physically or makes any utterance, gesture, or display designed to outrage the sensibilities of the group." See KY R.S. §525.150.

Importantly, the statute at issue is enforceable. See *Hartman v. Thompson*, 931 F. 3d 471 (6th Cir. 2019)(recognizing Kentucky State Trooper's right to effect an arrest under this statute of protesters disrupting a lawful gathering).

Virtually every State in the Union has a similar statute. Here in Louisiana, the statute is part of our "Disturbing the Peace" statute, La. R.S. 14:103. Specifically, §103(A)(6) criminalizes, "Interruption of any lawful assembly of people." Louisiana's statute was found to be constitutional as well. See *State v. Encalade*, 505 So. 2d 87 (La. App. 4th Cir.), *writ denied*, 508 So. 2d 63 (La. 1987).

Importantly, the First Amendment to the United States Constitution grants Americans not only the right to Freedom of Speech, but also "the right of the people to peaceably assemble," among other rights.

No one has a Constitutional Right to interfere with the rights of others to peacefully assemble. As the United States Supreme Court once observed, "The Right of Free Speech does not embrace a right to snuff out the free speech of others." *Red Lion Broadcasting Co., Inc. v. FCC*, 395 U.S. 367 (1969).

The right of people (or even the Government for that matter) to assemble and speak includes the complimentary right to exclude from the gathering those who express a contrary message. See *Hurley v. Irish-American Gay, Lesbian and Bisexual Group of Boston, Inc.*, 515 U.S. 557 (1995). See also, *Sistrunk v. City of Strongville*, 99 F. 3d 194 (6th Cir. 1996). There are plenty of other cases along these lines, but I don't want this Chapter to read more like a legal brief than it already does.

FAKE NEWS EXPOSED ABOUT TRUMP

The simple fact is President Trump did not argue the people of this Country had no right to protest him. That claim was simply untrue. His legal team argued only that Trump and his supporters rights to assemble and Trump's right to say what he said at the 2016 rally were protected by the First Amendment. President Trump's legal team was right.

Commentary: Some in the Fake News Media believe the far left has the right to disrupt the lawful gatherings of everyone else. There is simply no other explanation for this mentality that protesters get to infiltrate a political gathering and then shout, scream, shout down and otherwise disrupt it. Who in their right mind would think that conduct is proper? Worse, how warped must one's mind be to think the ones who are out of line are the people trying to stop the unlawful disruption of a political rally so the people lawfully gathered at the rally may exercise their First Amendment Rights? This is how low the left, and many of their lackeys in the Fake News Media, sunk. (The left's meltdown over Twitter™ being sold to Elon Musk tells you all you need to know about their disdain for Free Speech.) At least now we know.

24

SENATE COMMITTEE INVESTIGATING TRUMP ASSOCIATES?

No, wrong again.

THE FAKE NEWS

In June 2017, during the height of the phony "Russia-collusion" misinformation campaign, a U.S. Senate Committee began an investigation of a Russian government investment fund and ties to Trump campaign associate Anthony Scaramucci.

Who Pushed the Fake News?

CNN published the story on its website on June 22, 2017. The story was retracted and deleted. A link to the story does not exist. This writer could not locate the article in any archives. The story is reconstructed using some of the articles written challenging *CNN*'s Fake News.

Breitbart published an article on June 23, 2017, outlining the claims made by *CNN* in its now-retracted article. See "*Very Fake News: After Breitbart Investigation, CNN Retracts Conspiracy Theory Hit Piece Attacking Trump Associates*

Over Russian Fund," June 23, 2017, *breitbart.com.*

The *CNN* story was based on a single anonymous source, of course (as readers probably already guessed). Based on this anonymous source, *CNN* claimed the Senate Intelligence Committee was investigating Anthony Scaramucci, SkyBridge Capital founder, Trump supporter and Trump transition team member over what was characterized in the article as a "meeting" with the Russian investment fund's chief executive, Kirill Dmitriev. As reported by *Breitbart, CNN* wrote:

"Scaramucci, the founder of SkyBridge Capital, minimized his January meeting with Dmitriev in the resort town of Davos, Switzerland, at the celebrated annual gathering of the World Economic Forum. Scaramucci had met Dmitriev at previous Davos meetings, although at the gathering in January, Scaramucci was expecting to be named White House liaison to the business community."

The *CNN* article also claimed:

"The source said the Senate intelligence committee is investigating the Russian fund in connection with its examination of discussions between White House adviser Jared Kushner and the head of a prominent Russian bank. The bank, Vnesheconombank, or VEB, oversees the fund, which has ties to several Trump advisers. Both the bank and the fund have been covered since 2014 by sanctions restricting U.S. business dealings."

See the *Breitbart* article cited above.

THE TRUTH

The story was not true. There was no Senate investigation into Scaramucci. Scaramucci had no "connections" to the Russian investment fund. *CNN* retracted the story and issued an apology to Anthony Scaramucci.

On June 23, 2017, *CNN* retracted the story and replaced it with an "Editor's Note" stating the following:

"On June 22, 2017, CNN.com published a story connecting Anthony Scaramucci with investigations into the Russian Direct Investment Fund.

That story did not meet CNN's editorial standards and has been retracted. Links to the story have been disabled. CNN apologizes to Mr. Scaramucci."

See *CNN*, "*Editor's Note*," June 23, 2017, *cnn.com*.

A *CNN* reporter and two editors resigned over the retracted story. See *Business Insider*, "*3 CNN staffers out over retracted Russia investigation story*," June 26, 2017, *businessinsider.com*.

The Independent published a good breakdown of the Fake News on June 26, 2017, *independent.co.uk*:

CNN deletes false story on Trump ally's links to Russia: 'It was a massive f*** up'

A good explanation of how the phony *CNN* story was published, and the mistakes made, are provided by *The Washington Post* in an article published on August 17, 2017, *washingtonpost.com*:

The story behind a retracted CNN report on the Trump campaign and Russia

This Fake News story is more proof positive of why stories should not be published based on anonymous sources. As *The Washington Post* reports in the article cited above the single anonymous source did not corroborate the story completely when contacted after the story ran. One single anonymous source should never be enough to base any story on. Period. One would think these guys would learn that.

Commentary: How many times do Fake News Media run stories sourced only by anonymous sources? (Endlessly.) How many times do the stories prove to be Fake News? (Repeatedly.) This is one of the rare cases where there were consequences for the people peddling the Fake News. Retracting the story is commendable, though one would expect the retraction to state the story was not true. Demanding resignations from three people associated with the Fake News story actually seems harsh. Fake News Media could put a swift end to the phony stories by halting publication of any story based solely on anonymous sources. But, they are not going to do that.

25

TRUMP EPA CLEARS PESTICIDE AFTER MEETING WITH DOW CHEMICAL CEO?

No, there was no "meeting."

THE FAKE NEWS

Scott Pruitt, the head of the federal Environmental Protection Agency (EPA) in the Trump Administration approved the use of a chemical, chlorpyrifos, on crops despite claims ingesting the chemical can interfere with the brain development of infants and fetuses, but only after meeting with the CEO of Dow Chemical, the company which manufactures chlorpyrifos.

Who Pushed the Fake News?

The Associated Press in an article published on June 27, 2017, *apnews.com*:

EPA chief met with Dow CEO before deciding on pesticide ban

(Please note: The original article was corrected. The headline above is from the original article.)

The original article claimed:

"The Trump administration's top environmental official met privately with the chief executive of Dow Chemical shortly before reversing his agency's push to ban a widely used pesticide after health studies showed it can harm children's brains, according to records obtained by The Associated Press."

(The original article was corrected and this writer could not locate the entire original article in its unedited form. This quote is from the original article, as quoted in a *Breitbart* article exposing the Fake News and appears word-for-word in the corrected article as well. See *Breitbart*, *"Fake News: Associated Press Engulfed in CNN-Level Scandal As It Covers Up Invention of Imaginary Pruitt Meeting,"* June 30, 2017, *Breitbart.com*.)

The original article stated EPA Administrator Scott Pruitt met with the Dow Chemical CEO for about half an hour in March 2017 at a hotel in Houston, Texas during an energy industry conference and 20 days later Pruitt made his decision to allow the chemical to be used. See *Breitbart* article cited above.

THE TRUTH

The head of the EPA, Scott Pruitt, and the CEO of Dow Chemical, Andrew Liveris, did not meet for half an hour at a hotel in Houston, Texas. The meeting was canceled due to scheduling conflicts. See *Breitbart*, *"Fake News: Associated Press Engulfed in CNN-Level Scandal As It Covers Up Invention of Imaginary Pruitt Meeting,"* June 30, 2017, *Breitbart.com*; the corrected *Associated Press* article and *The Hill*, *"Media errors give Trump fresh ammunition,"* July 4, 2017, *thehill.com*.

As *The Hill* acknowledged in the article entitled, *"Media errors give Trump fresh ammunition,"* on July 4, 2017, the AP article about the meeting that did not happen "insinuated" that the head of the EPA made the decision to allow the use of the chemical "under pressure from a corporate lobbying campaign."

But, the story, and its insinuations, were not true. As *Breitbart* put it:

FAKE NEWS: ASSOCIATED PRESS ENGULFED IN CNN-LEVEL SCANDAL AS IT COVERS UP INVENTION OF IMAGINARY PRUITT MEETING

A spokeswoman for the EPA told *Breitbart News* that the AP article is "inaccurate and misleading" since the private meeting did not take place and that the AP refused to correct the article "despite multiple attempts to provide the Associated Press with the facts . . .."

The Associated Press eventually did correct the article and rephrased the language in the article to state the meeting was "slated" to happen, but did not, due to scheduling conflicts. See the corrected *Associated Press* article. The corrected article also includes an introductory paragraph outlining the errors in the original article.

Simply stated, the AP story was wrong. Insinuating the CEO of Dow Chemical somehow strongarmed the EPA chief at a private meeting into denying petitions to ban the use of this pesticide was simply wrong.

Commentary: *The Associated Press* reported on this private meeting (which never happened), and insinuated the CEO of Dow Chemical somehow persuaded the chief of the EPA to deny petitions to ban this pesticide all based off of schedules obtained from the EPA. This means the AP ran this story without even requesting comment from either the EPA or the CEO of Dow Chemical. The AP claimed a meeting occurred, when it did not, and implied the EPA chief made his decision on this pesticide based on that non-existent meeting, without asking any of the individuals or organizations involved anything about the meeting itself. How simple would it have been for *The Associated Press* to reach out to the EPA and Dow Chemical? After dropping this ball, the

FAKE NEWS EXPOSED ABOUT TRUMP

AP then waited basically one week to correct the story. If that is not Fake News what is?

There is more to this Fake News story. What about that chemical, chlorpyrifos? Do some research on that pesticide and you might conclude it is scary stuff, particularly for pregnant women and small children. This will be the result if you read the news media reports about it. There is a little more to it than that though. What follows is short recap of the procedural history of the EPA's handling of the petition to ban this pesticide. This history is taken from the Federal Appeals Court decision in *League of United Latin American Citizens v. Regan*, 996 F. 3d 673 decided in 2021.

The Fake News Media lambasts the EPA decision in March 2017, in the early stages of the Trump Administration, to deny the petition to ban chlorpyrifos, but what they rarely mention is the petition to ban chlorpyrifos was filed in *September 2007* by the Pesticide Action Network North America and the National Resources Defense Council. This petition bounced around the EPA during the entire *two terms* of President Obama's administration. The Obama Administration EPA only finally issued a "proposed rule" to revoke the pesticide's tolerances (basically to ban its use) after the United States Court of Appeals for the Ninth Circuit issued a *Writ of Mandamus*, in August 2015, ordering the EPA to provide a response to the petition. (A *Writ of Mandamus* is an extraordinary writ used, in this context, to have a Court order a government official to take some sort of action to fulfill his or her duties. See *Cornell Law School, Legal Information Institute, Mandamus, law.cornell.edu*. The standards for issuing such a writ are difficult to meet, so the action of the court ordering the EPA to make a decision is a good indication the EPA drug its feet.)

Despite the order of the Federal Appeals Court, the EPA still did not rule on the petition until November 2016, when the EPA indicated it would revoke the tolerances for the pesticide (essentially banning it). The EPA indicated it ruled as it did because of the Federal Appeals Court's orders demanding it make a decision and that it actually needed more time to complete further studies to issue a final rule. The EPA indicated in the order, however, that the decision was not final and may be revisited.

Then, in 2017, the Trump Administration took over and the petition to revoke the pesticide's tolerances (which would essentially ban it) was denied, thereby allowing the pesticide to continue to be used.

Interested readers may read a more comprehensive recitation of the history of this pesticide, the procedural history of the petition to ban it and the EPA's decision in the Ninth Circuit Court of Appeals Opinion on the case in the Federal Reporter at 996 F. 3d 673. (The tortured administrative history of the petition to ban the pesticide is covered in the dissent. That history starts on page 88 of the opinion and runs to page 101.)

Ultimately, the United States Court of Appeal for the Ninth Circuit ruled the EPA incorrectly denied the petition to ban the pesticide. (The dissenting opinion in the case is written by Judge Jay Bybee, who was a professor at Louisiana State University's Paul M. Hebert Law Center back when I was in law school there in the mid-1990s. You may remember Judge Bybee from his time at the United States Department of Justice in the administration of George W. Bush. Judge Bybee, then with the Office of Legal Counsel of the DOJ, co-authored the famous "*torture memos*" which supposedly formed the basis of alleged mistreatment of detainees in the "War on Terror." The legal profession can be a small world. Despite all of the bad press surrounding the "torture memos," Judge Bybee is a great guy and a brilliant judge.)

The point is the Fake News Media viciously attacked the Trump Administration for denying the petition to ban the pesticide, but that same Fake News Media levied little or no criticism against the Obama Administration for sitting on the petition for two entire presidential terms and only making a decision because a Federal Appeals Court ordered it to. See how that works? The Obama Administration does nothing to ban this pesticide for nearly a decade, but Obama and company get little or no criticism for doing nothing. The Trump

Administration takes decisive action, albeit not what the media wanted, and gets pilloried. This disparate treatment of Obama versus Trump is another hallmark of Fake News.

Meanwhile, if you study up on this pesticide, you will probably rest a bit easier knowing it is no longer in use. Dow Chemical, the manufacturer of chlorpyrifos, announced in early 2020 it planned to stop producing the chemical by the end of that year (2020) due to decreasing demand. See *The Guardian*, "*Largest maker of pesticide linked to brain damage in kids to stop producing chemical,*" February 6, 2020, *theguardian.com*. The following year the United States Court of Appeal for the Ninth Circuit issued its Opinion ordering the EPA to cancel the pesticide (what a courageous decision, ordering the EPA to pull the pesticide after the manufacturer announced it would quit producing it). A few months later, the EPA announces the ban on the agricultural use of the pesticide. See *U.S. PIRG*, "*Victory: EPA bans pesticide linked to brain damage in children,*" September 17, 2021, *uspirg.org*. (Another courageous decision, eh? Well, the EPA could have asked the United States Supreme Court to review the case, I suppose.) Nevertheless, for what it is worth, I am glad this chemical is not being sprayed on crops anymore. The EPA under the Trump Administration probably got that call wrong, but a non-existent meeting that never happened with Dow Chemical's CEO had nothing to do with it.

26

Conclusion

The Fake News stories highlighted in this book are a sliver of the Fake News spread by the so-called "Mainstream Media." There are many more Fake News stories told about President Trump, the Trump Administration, the Trump campaign, the Trump family and Trump supporters. If one widens the net to include gun owners, religious folks or conservatives generally, the growth in Fake News stories is incredible. If one widens the search further to include topics of concern, such as the Right to Bear Arms, abortion, taxes, the environment, animal rights, hunting, tariffs, trade, etc..., the number of Fake News stories is virtually impossible to catalog.

Hopefully, those who read this book will be empowered to think on their own, do their own research, reach their own conclusions and never take any report from the Fake News Media at face value. Maybe some of the Fake News and media misinformation upsets you. (It probably should.) Use those emotions to motivate you to search for truth, far beyond the publications of the legacy media.

Mostly, I hope the Fake News stories exposed in this book compel readers to get their information from as diverse a list of sources as possible. As former President and Founding Father Thomas Jefferson once said "Whenever the people are well-informed, they can be trusted with their own government."

Volume Two of *Fake News Exposed about Trump* covers another twenty-nine (29) Fake News Media lies, misrepresentations, half-truths, embellishments and fabrications about former President Trump, his family, his businesses and his Presidential Administration. While Volume Three covers thirty (30) more. If you enjoyed this book, you will enjoy Volumes Two and Three as well. I hope you will give those a look.

Once again, please visit my website, DanielRStreet.com for more information about my books, for news and updates about upcoming books. Visit my substack at danielrstreet.substack.com for breakdowns of Fake News stories, Media misinformation and other nonsense of the day. Also, please join my email list at https://www.danielrstreet.com/v1b/. Visit this link to sign up and *receive a free bonus chapter* only available to my readers. If you enjoyed this book you will enjoy all of the rest of my platforms as well.

Finally, thank you for purchasing this book. Nothing is more gratifying to an author than people reading his or her book. If you enjoyed this book and found it informative, please take a moment to visit Amazon and leave a review. Your feedback and support are very important. Thanks again and best wishes to you all.

Daniel R. Street, Monroe, Louisiana.

About the Author

Daniel R. Street is an attorney with over two decades of experience handling civil litigation in State and Federal Court in Louisiana. He avidly follows American politics and is deeply concerned our Country is undermined by the suppression of Free Speech. He is a hunter, gun owner, fisherman and Christian. He and his family live in Monroe, Louisiana.

You can connect with me on:
- https://www.danielrstreet.com
- https://twitter.com/DanielRStreet1

Subscribe to my newsletter:
- https://danielrstreet.substack.com

Made in the USA
Columbia, SC
04 August 2023